INCREDIBLE
JOURNEYS

NIGEL

MARVEN

INCREDIBLE JOURNEYS

*Featuring the World's
Greatest Animal Travellers*

BBC BOOKS

For Jenny, with love.
Our 'Incredible Journey' is just beginning

No natural history series or book would be possible without the help of scores of biologists and naturalists. Sadly, the confines of this page means that I cannot mention them all by name, but I thank all of them for their faxes, e-mails, conversations by phone and help when accompanying the film crews in the field.

The *Incredible Journeys* team from the BBC Natural History unit worked tirelessly for two years, often under the greatest of pressures, and their help and commitment to the making of the series was extraordinary. My thanks to them all; Andy Byatt, Lisa Connaire, Louise Dawe-Lane, Matt Thompson and Nigel Williams. The cameramen and post production specialists also gave their all and I'm indebted to Andrew Anderson, Neil Bromhall, Rod Clarke, Peter Hicks, Mike Marshall, Suzanne Outlaw, Lucy Rutherford, Sinclair Stammers and Vince Wright.

I am also grateful to the team at BBC Books. As a first-time author I could never have written this book without the support of my commissioning editor, Sheila Ableman, and my editor, Charlotte Lochhead, who was patient and enthusiastic even when I made changes at the last moment and pushed deadlines to the limit. Paula Cahill co-ordinated the gathering of the stunning photos for Martin Hendry to use in designing the book. Many of these were specially taken during the making of the series and I am indebted to all the photographers for their efforts. I must also thank Mark Flowers for his help with the rattlesnake chapter.

I am particularly indebted to assistant producer, Stephen Dunleavy, cameramen, Alan Hayward, Gavin Thurston and Mark Payne-Gill and film editor David McCormick. Out of the creative fervour of making films I have developed lasting friendships with all of them.

Approximate conversions metric
to imperial:
25 millimetres = 1 inch
2.5 centimetres = 1 inch
1 metre = just over 3 feet
1 kilogram = just over 2 lb
1 kilometre = ⅝ mile
(8 kilometres = 5 miles)

To convert centigrade temperatures
to Fahrenheit, subtract 32 degrees,
then multiply by 5 and divide by 9

This book is published to accompany the television series entitled *Incredible Journeys* which was first broadcast in 1997.

Published by BBC Books,
an imprint of BBC Worldwide Publishing.
BBC Worldwide Limited, Woodlands,
80 Wood Lane, London W12 0TT

First published 1997
© Nigel Marven 1997
The moral right of the author has been asserted

ISBN 0 563 38736 X

Designed by Martin Hendry
Maps by Line and Line

Set in Spectrum
Printed and bound in Great Britain by Butler & Tanner, Frome
Colour separations by Radstock Reproductions Ltd, Midsomer Norton
Jacket printed by Lawrence Allen Ltd, Weston-super-Mare

CONTENTS

INTRODUCTION

OF THE MANY intriguing aspects of the natural world, perhaps none is more awe-inspiring than the incredible journeys that some creatures regularly undertake, year after year, generation after generation. This book, and the film series which it accompanies, follows six very different species whose navigational skills, persistence and endurance, sometimes in the face of seemingly impossible odds, are truly amazing. These animals are not, of course, the only ones for whom travelling is a way of life, but I chose them over other potential candidates because each has something special.

The initial inspiration for me to tell the stories of animal travellers came from one tiny bird. One of my earliest memories is of a barn swallow, swooping low over my head in pursuit of insects that I'd flushed from the grass. The bird flashed into the dark recesses of a farm shed and, as I waited by the door, I could hear the clamour of its chicks as they were being fed. I excitedly babbled what I'd seen to my father who told me something I could scarcely believe: the birds I was watching in southern England would spend the winter nearly 10,000 kilometres away.

The barn swallow is one of the most familiar birds in the world. One reason for this is its confiding nature, which has led to a close association with people. From Stone Age times to the present day swallows have chosen to nest almost exclusively in our dwellings, from mud huts to concrete cowsheds. They breed over much of Europe, Asia and North America. The birds spend only half of the year in these northern latitudes and this is another reason why they attract attention.

The way swallows appear in the British spring and disappear in autumn has always intrigued people. It was once believed that their wings were too fragile to carry them across continents and oceans, and that instead they flew to the moon. Some scientists in the sixteenth and seventeenth centuries became convinced that swallows spent the winter cocooned in mud at the bottom of ponds. This idea arose because of the birds' habits of flying low over lakes and ponds, and of huddling close together in reed-beds on the margins of water.

In Baja California the author encounters a grey whale. Here at the San Ignacio lagoon, where the greys come to breed, 'friendly' whales have been approaching small boats for over 20 years.

Today we know that swallows spend the winter in the southern hemisphere: but this migration is just as amazing as these fanciful ideas, and would have been equally unimaginable to those early naturalists. It was bird ringing that provided irrefutable proof that twice a year swallows do indeed make an intercontinental odyssey, and that those fragile-looking wings do carry them over oceans, mountains and deserts.

The sheer magnitude of their migration and the problems these tiny birds must overcome was brought home to us during filming. We followed the autumn exodus as far as the Sahara by ferry and road, covering thousands of kilometres. For two days in the Camargue in southern France we couldn't film: there were gale-force winds and even when these let up the camera lenses were spotted with droplets from sudden squalls of freezing rain. In periods of calm the swallows flew close to the ground, snatching up any insects they could find. Their journey had faltered but as soon as the weather improved these tenacious travellers pressed southwards once more.

Farther south in Morocco, we and the birds again had to contend with the same problems in the Sahara, the world's largest desert. In early October the temperature was 35 degrees centigrade, and while he filmed swallows slaking their thirst at an oasis, cameraman Mark Payne-Gill guzzled 3 litres of mineral water a day.

For the last part of the swallow's migration, we also travelled by air, of course in a jet. Our aircraft weighed 396 tonnes and was 70 metres long, whereas that little bird I had seen so many years earlier, and all its relatives and descendants now following the same route, are only 18 centimetres long and a mere 22 grams. Our flight to South Africa was fuelled by 100,000 kilos of fuel; the swallows' energy came only from insects which they snatched en route. The efficiency of the fuel consumption of birds is astounding. (No calculations have been done specifically for a swallow, but the blackpoll warbler does the equivalent of 720,000 miles to the gallon/250,000 kilometres to the litre.)

Our destination was the Mkze game reserve in the province of Natal. One day as Mark and I waited in a hide, there was an ear-splitting snort as a magnificent white rhino lumbered towards the waterhole to wallow. Before they were dunked, clouds of shiny green flies took off from its hide. Suddenly a barn swallow appeared and swept through the insects, snapping up one or two in its beak, before skimming the water surface to drink. As I thought about the journey that this tiny bird, barely the size of my clenched fist, had achieved, the hairs on the back of my neck tingled. There was a slim possibility (very slim as over 200 million barn swallows overwinter in Africa) that this was one of the swallows we had filmed fledging from a farm in southern England. There it had pursued insects around cattle; now it was hawking for them around big game.

I chose the swallows' journey because the spectacular landscapes along the route equal those overflown by any other birds. But the barn swallow doesn't travel the farthest; that honour goes to the Arctic tern which covers about 30,000 kilometres from the Arctic to the Antarctic and back each year. The second story about caribou trekkers of North America does feature a champion. It has recently been discovered that on their mass migrations for food and to traditional calving grounds they walk further than any mammal on the planet. I also chose caribou because we could take advantage of the work of pioneering biologist Serge Couturier, who has followed the herds over thousands of kilometres of tundra.

The pair of helicopters buzzed low over the vast and featureless landscape. Cameraman Gavin Thurston, assistant producer Matt Thompson and I flew behind Serge and his scientific team. Somewhere below us there were three-quarters of a million caribou. We couldn't see one because the animals were scattered across an area of Quebec larger than that of Europe. Their sombre pelts also blended perfectly with the muted tones of the tundra so the inexperienced filming contingent were constantly being hoodwinked by herds of boulders high on a hill. But at last, after a two-hour search, the lead helicopter hovered high above an aggregation of 20,000 caribou.

I had never seen so many mammals in one place. The brown tide seemed to flow over the barren landscape, many of the deer browsing as they walked, snatching up mouthfuls of leaves from dwarf willows. Caribou have always been hunted by the native peoples of Canada and their general movements have been known since time immemorial, but looking down at the dense mass it seemed impossible to keep track of individuals. So how had Serge managed to do so?

The answer was that one or two of the caribou had been fitted with a plastic necklace containing a radio transmitter. In this way they could be tracked continuously by satellite and as a result their route and the distance travelled could be plotted on a map. In this way Serge made his amazing discovery, finding that the perambulations of a female caribou took her an astonishing 9000 kilometres in just one year. Even more astonishing was that her new-born calf tagged alongside and covered the same distance.

Other animals find their way to destinations they've never been to before without parental help. Freshwater eels do this when they migrate, and in a series and book of this kind I felt it was essential to include their migration, a journey which is as mysterious as it is incredible. To film these creatures, the assistance of eel fishermen was as invaluable as that of scientists – the fishermen have to have some idea of when and where eels travel or they would go out of business. Tom Osborne is one of the most experienced in Australia. He specializes in catching the short-finned eel that lives there. I asked him when the upstream run of young eels, or elvers, would begin and he told me he could predict it by a complex alchemy of water flow, phase of the moon and season but, most importantly, by his instinct.

Cameraman Mark Payne-Gill and I hoped to film the pencil-sized fish ascending a 3-metre-high concrete dam. First I had to persuade Tom to put traps only at the top of the dam – his catch wouldn't be less, but at least the elvers wouldn't be caught before we could film them. Then for three whole nights we watched and waited. On the first night Tom put his hand into the water and said the current was too strong for the elvers to swim against. On the second he scrutinized the cloudless night sky and told us the light of the moon would put them off. On the third night the water flow had dropped and the moon was obscured by clouds; conditions were perfect but we still only saw two dozen elvers.

We decided to persevere for one more night, and just after dusk it happened at last. Hundreds of elvers began to surge from the river, and soon there was a chain of thousands of them squirming and wriggling their way to the top of the dam. Each time one made it we were secretly relieved if it swam to the side or beneath Tom's trap. We filmed all through the night – the moon was bright, and our lights brighter still, but the elvers kept climbing. Elated, we laughed with Tom. His confidence had belied the fact that predicting elver runs is like forecasting the weather – an imprecise art.

These elvers would penetrate far upstream to colonize ponds, lakes and billabongs. If they escaped the attention of predators, they would stay and mature in fresh water for fifteen years before migrating to their ocean birthplace to lay eggs. Scientists have never found these spawning grounds and their exact position remains a mystery.

Until January 1975 this was also true for the destination of the only insect traveller chosen for the series. No other insect can match the monarch butterfly in terms of distance travelled, numbers of individuals involved and feats of pinpoint navigation. It had been known for many years that the monarchs of the eastern United States migrate south at the end of the summer, but where they went was one of the great unsolved puzzles of natural history.

The discovery of their refuge came about as a result of forty years' painstaking work by Canadian and American scientists. Butterflies can't be ringed like birds, but they can be tagged by scraping some of the scales off one wing and attaching a sticky label bearing an address to contact if the butterfly is recovered. In 1951 at the outset of the project three thousand monarchs were tagged and, although only seven were recovered, one had travelled over 2000 kilometres away. The tantalizing possibilities spurred the scientists on to even greater endeavours. Professor Fred Urquart and his wife Nora spearheaded the project, and with the help of volunteers directed the tagging of more than 400,000 monarchs. On a map of North America, the Urquarts drew lines between release and recapture points and by the early 1970s these lines pointed unequivocally to Mexico.

Here the search zeroed in on the trans-volcanic range just west of Mexico City. In these mountains, amongst groves of oyamel pine, the mystery of the monarch was solved: the butterflies were present in their millions. As I struggled to the monarchs' high-altitude winter hideaway I experienced much the same thrill that the Urquarts had, twenty years before. At over 3000 metres my breath was already short, but the spectacle before me took it completely away. In every direction the view was filled with these majestic bright orange butterflies. Soaring, gliding and floating, they seemed to fill the whole sky whether I looked straight up, ahead, to the left or to the right. They made solid structures as well: the millions hanging from the trees formed huge clusters which totally obscured the trunks. It is hardly surprising that assistant producer Stephen Dunleavy and cameraman Rod Clarke spent over three weeks in these mountains, shooting 300 minutes of spectacular footage which, sadly, we had to condense to less than seven in the finished programme. Even so, the magic remains inescapable.

Unlike the monarch butterfly, the destination of the grey whale has been well known for a long time: people knew the whereabouts of these creatures because they were a commodity to be hunted. Many whales migrate – indeed, they are the oceans' champion long-distance navigators – but I chose Pacific greys for three reasons. Firstly, they are the only whales to hug the shoreline, so we wouldn't be restricted to a film of featureless ocean, but could show the coastal landmarks of North America that they swam past. Secondly, grey whales have been officially protected for some fifty years so there are fair numbers to film. But thirdly, and most importantly, since 1976 some grey whales in the breeding lagoons have exhibited extraordinary behaviours.

Throughout the filming our aim, wherever possible, was to go right alongside the animal travellers so that viewers could experience the journey for themselves. We could do this with the grey as it is unique amongst the larger whales in that it allows and even encourages close human contact. The individuals who do this are known as 'friendlies'. The first observations were of an adult cow who approached small boats and pushed her head out of the lagoon. She even rubbed her great body against the hulls. Over the years, more and more whales have become 'friendlies'. Some cows even lead their newborn calves to boats and nudge them closer to the awe-struck passengers.

This phenomenon is best seen in February or March in the San Ignacio breeding lagoon in Baja California, Mexico, although some greys are still friendly in northern waters. No one is certain why they respond in this way. Perhaps they come to investigate because a boat engine produces underwater sounds at frequencies similar to their own contact calls, or maybe they simply like the feel of the hull or human hands on their skins. Whatever the reason, a close encounter with these creatures is unforgettable.

As I leaned over the side of our small boat a 12-metre, 30 tonne cow languidly lifted her vast head out of the water. Gently at first, and with some trepidation, I rubbed my hands over her skin, but she soon lost interest and slipped back under the water. Chris Peterson, a whale biologist, said I'd hold her attention longer with a rougher caress, and when she was ready she would probably come back. A three-week-old calf played by her side, sometimes rolling on to her mother's broad back. To record these intimate moments from only centimetres away, cameraman Andrew Anderson hung over the side so his lens was between the two whales. I held my breath as this time the calf came towards me. Water streamed off her head and as she surfaced the rivulets glistened in the sunshine. I rubbed along her lips and she opened her great mouth, encouraging me actually to push my hand inside. I felt the stiff bristles through which these whales filter food, and actually stroked her huge pink tongue. It was an extraordinary and thrilling sensation.

One creature whose mouth no one would want to put a hand into is the western diamondback rattlesnake. Like the caribou, this is an animal whose movements have been minutely tracked using up-to-date satellite technology.

Using data from transmitters, tiny enough to be inserted under the skin of a snake, scientists Dave Duvall and Steve Bopres have shown that the slitherings of the western diamondback are not random. In Arizona's Sonoran Desert, the reptiles they studied actually navigated to precise destinations. One female was found in the same pack-rat nest for three summers in succession: every autumn she travelled over 4 kilometres back from the feeding grounds to a favoured site for hibernation, where she joined others of her kind in the labyrinth of clefts and crevices in a rocky bluff.

We intended to film the journeys of this population of rattlesnakes. Nothing seemed amiss when producer Andy Byatt and I went on our first reconnaissance trip. Freshly emerged from hibernation, large numbers of adult rattlesnakes basked and courted in the sunshine, apparently oblivious to us and to the gopher tortoises that trundled by to browse on patches of spring flowers. Flashes of iridescent green and purple zipped in and out of higher blooms as Costa's hummingbirds refuelled with nectar. The rocky ridge on which we were standing was dominated by giant saguaro cacti, some of them centuries old. All around this sanctuary we could see the threats facing the desert. Vast areas are being swallowed up by new golf courses and retirement towns. Even though this harsh environment doesn't get as much publicity as the rainforest, its future, and that of the creatures it supports, could be just as bleak.

The nature reserve where we stood should have been secure, but underfoot there was an invidious threat. Like most of the Sonoran Desert, alien grasses originally introduced as fodder for cattle cover the ground. Where, in the past, there were natural firebreaks of dry, bare ground now there is a dangerous, flammable carpet. So when a fire breaks out, instead of stuttering to a halt it rampages through the desert.

A terrific blaze ravaged hundreds of square kilometres, including the rocky ridge with the rattlesnakes, just three months after we'd left. The saguaros and many other native plants that are not fire adapted were killed outright and it will take at least a century before these majestic saguaros rise again from the scene of devastation.

In the short term, however, many of the rattlesnakes that Dave Duvall is studying escaped the blaze by retreating underground. In due course the survivors emerged to explore a new landscape, charred and blackened; Dave even saw their tracks in ashes still hot to the touch in this devastated habitat. The long term survival of this population of snakes is uncertain, but at the very least their annual journeys will be disrupted for the next few years and this was what we needed to film. We had to turn our cameras and lenses to another rattlesnake population, which at least for now, still slithers in the shadow of ancient saguaros.

The journeys of all six animal travellers – swallows, caribou, eels, monarch butterflies, grey whales and rattlesnakes – are truly incredible. Even in this age of faxes, computers and super information highways, I still think it is nothing short of miraculous when I see the first swallow of spring. Modern technology might seem to rival the abilities of these creatures, but no machine surpasses their astonishing feats.

THE SWALLOW'S ODYSSEY

WITH A FINAL wriggle, the tiny creature shakes himself free from the egg. Unseeing eyes bulge from a head that seems outsized compared with the rest of his body. He's naked except for a few tufts of damp down plastered against his skin; these will soon dry and become fluffy. Yet this pink apparition has powers beyond imagination. If he can avoid the hazards ahead, he will complete an epic journey of nearly 10,000 kilometres before he's five months old. Even now he's programmed for an odyssey that will take him across forests and deserts, mountains and oceans. He has an internal clock to tell him when to go and a whole array of inbuilt navigation systems to help him find his way. He is a barn swallow *(Hirundo rustica)* – a bird that, even fully grown, is barely the size of a man's clenched fist.

This cock swallow is the last to hatch out of a brood of five. He lies flat out on a feather, exhausted after breaking out of the egg. He and his siblings are high up in a barn in southern England. Their mud nest is attached to a wooden rafter and lined with second-hand white feathers, moulted by the poultry in the farmyard and collected by the parent swallows. The feathers act as a duvet to keep the swallow chicks insulated. At first all our cock bird can do is feebly lift his head and open his beak to be fed. He can't even generate his own body heat, so must rely on his mother to keep him warm. For the first few days she rarely leaves the nest, so her mate is left with the task of finding food.

The parent birds look very much the same, but sitting tight on the nest the female is hidden in the shadows. As the male comes in and out with food, he shows how strikingly handsome and well designed swallows are. His forehead and throat are a rich chestnut brown, while creamy white underparts emphasize the steel-blue of his back which shimmers in a shaft of sunlight as he makes dashing swoops through the barn. Built for agility and speed in the air, he has a short body and neck, with long wings that reduce drag and maximize lift. He achieves precision turning and braking with the help of his long tail. In the coming weeks he'll need all his aerial skills, as swallows feed on virtually nothing but winged insects and he must fly like a dervish to supply his mate and brood.

When they hatch, the swallow chicks weigh a mere 1.5 grams, but, crammed with food, they gain up to 2 grams a day. At about a week old their eyes are fully open and there is a stubble of black feather tips breaking through their skin. At this stage they're all mouth, and what a mouth it is. Their gaping beaks reveal bright yellow throats which in the gloom of the barn are perfect targets for their parents returning with food. Now that they can just about regulate their own body temperature the chicks don't need to be brooded unless it's cool, so the female is free to help keep those mouths filled.

A total of six pairs of swallows have chosen to nest on the farm. Unless it's cold and wet there are always one or more parent birds criss-crossing the sky in the search for insects. The farm has cows and horses which attract larger flies, a pond and ancient hedgerows to provide myriads of mayflies, midges, fungus gnats and the like, so there is plenty of food to go round.

The parent birds rarely forage farther than 300 metres away from the nest. Unless their prey is very large, they make many catches per trip. The insects are packed away in their throat to form a food ball for the young. The weather is warm and the hunting is good, so the parents return with food up to twenty times an hour. In just one day the brood of five chicks put away 6000 bluebottles, robber-flies, hover-flies and horse-flies. They will eat 150,000 insects before they leave the nest.

At twenty-one days old, our cock swallow and his nest-mates are shabby replicas of their parents. Their feathers and the nest are dusted with white fragments, the remains of the waxy sheaths that once protected their growing feathers. The young birds are old enough to fly, so today their parents don't go straight to them with food. To encourage their young to lift off they call insistently, and hover in front of the nest. Our cock bird is the bravest, or hungriest, and he is first away.

It's an inauspicious flying start – he reaches the top of an antiquated plough only a metre away! His brother and sisters soon find their wings as well, and the plough becomes the feeding station for the rest of that day. As they become more confident fliers, the young swallows venture farther afield, returning to the vicinity of the nest at night. They rely on provisions from their parents for another week or so but pursue their own insects as well. Our cock swallow catches his first just six days after reaching the plough's dizzy heights. A horsefly plunges its dagger-like mouthparts into the back of a horse. More by luck than judgement, our young swallow swoops close and interrupts the fly's meal of blood. The insect reacts fast, but not fast enough, and the last thing it sees is a broad, flat bill snapping shut. A fortunate catch – if the fast-moving horsefly hadn't been up to its proboscis in a vein, it would have been more than a match for an inexperienced swallow.

Although they don't realize it, the fledgelings' lives revolve around preparing themselves for their incredible journey. They spend the days practising their aerobatic skills, literally playing in the air. On one occasion our swallow and his sister repeatedly drop a tiny feather, catching it before it floats to the ground. It's hard to believe they made their shaky first flight just ten days before. Now they revel in an element that has become their own.

The youngsters learn how bursts of easy wingbeats can propel them into long curves or swoops, and how a flick of a wingtip can jink them onto prey. Even though their tails are stubbier than their parents', they're still so effective as rudders and air-brakes that, when they're flying at full speed, they can turn through 90 degrees in less than the length of their bodies, needing just 18 centimetres of air space. These manoeuvres could save their lives on the perilous journey ahead.

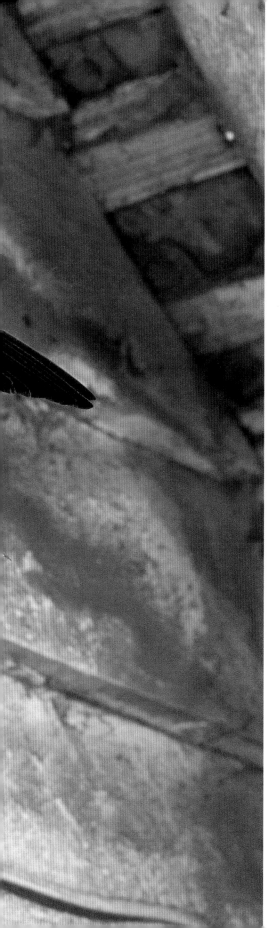

Each parent swallow may return to the nest up to twenty times an hour to provide the ever-hungry nestlings with food. The fledgelings compete noisily to be the one that receives a mouthful of insects.

The predatory hobby will feed its chicks on the flesh of small birds. This falcon acquires his home by requisitioning the abandoned nest of a crow or sparrowhawk or even a squirrel's drey.

As well as improving their prowess in the air, the young swallows must learn the landmarks around their home patch. From a vantage point high in the sky they look down and remember the alignment of hedgerows or the configuration of buildings in a village. If they survive, they'll need this knowledge to recognize their summer territory after six months away.

Swallows can have three clutches of eggs in a season. Our bird is from a late brood, so time is short. As well as mastering the skills of flight and making a mental map of where everything is, he also needs to feed up for the long flight south. During August and September, as he takes on extra fuel, his body mass will increase by 15 per cent. Other birds need to put on even more. Our swallow flits along hedgerows where willow warblers are gorging on berries. They have been insectivorous all summer long, but now they must achieve a remarkable feat and add up to half of their body weight in fat reserves. They can only do this by switching to a diet of fruits and berries, which are much richer in carbohydrates than insects. All this fuel is crucial because, unlike swallows which travel by day, feeding as they fly, willow warblers make non-stop night flights with refuelling breaks in between.

It's mid-September, and the days are getting shorter. From the annual calendar within their bodies the swallows receive a signal to leave the farm behind and begin their journey south for the winter. At first they fly at a leisurely pace, wandering in any direction, sometimes covering only 30 kilometres in a day. They can afford these peregrinations because insects are still plentiful, and by reconnoitring the surrounding countryside they may find new breeding territories to move to in the future if the present one changes for the worse. Every evening they must choose somewhere to roost: usually they sleep in a reed-bed, but a field of maize or a bed of willow will do. Soon they begin to travel more purposefully, orientating in a south-easterly direction and moving 100 kilometres or more in a day. Now swallows are pouring southwards from all over Britain and at favoured roosts hundreds, sometimes thousands, gather to sleep. The birds arrive in ones and twos but soon small groups form, which coalesce above the reeds into great gyrating clouds.

Sand martins, close relatives of swallows, form part of these flocks. They have brown backs and white underparts, with a brown band across the chest. At dusk it's hard to discern these details but the sand martins can still be distinguished by their short squarish tail and fluttery flight. Their wingbeats are reminiscent of fast-moving objects in an old, flickering film. The house martin, the final member of the swallow tribe found in Britain, has a blue-black head and wings, pure white underparts and striking white rump. Unlike the swallow, it has no patches of red on the head and throat and no blue chest band. House martins generally fly higher and more slowly than swallows, and have a short snub tail which gives them a stockier appearance. A few are hawking for insects when the swallows arrive at the marsh, but they disappear well before dusk. Unlike swallows and sand martins, house martins rarely roost in reed-beds, preferring to sleep in or under man-made structures, or amongst the leafy canopy of trees.

Another British bird, the swift, is not related to swallows at all, although it looks superficially similar. It's a uniform dark brown except for a whitish throat patch, with sickle-shaped wings and a short fork to the tail. The swift is never part of these late autumn gatherings, as it heads south much earlier in the year. Swifts fly faster than swallows, but even they can be caught by the aerobatic predator which haunts the huge concentration of birds now swirling above the reeds.

A hobby streaks across a sky dyed orange by the setting sun. This small falcon has a slate-grey back, buff underparts streaked with black and rich chestnut breeches. A face with a white throat and cheeks and a curving moustache of jet-black feathers give it a piratical look. In fact it mugged a kestrel earlier in the summer, stealing a mouse right from the larger bird's talons. But this was unusual – in spring and early summer its more usual food is insects, in particular dragonflies, which it catches on the wing.

From July onwards, the hobby focuses on feathered prey. Now in the twilight it uses a tactic that gives it the advantage of surprise. Scythe-shaped wings propel it fast and low right beneath the cloud of swallows and martins. The light is fading, and few of them notice the dark shape against the ground. They themselves are fully silhouetted against the sky. With talons outstretched, the hobby swoops upwards. Our swallow hears the air whistling over the hunter's wings. There's a blur of red feathers as the falcon extends its legs and four long-taloned toes. It cannons past our swallow to snatch another bird flying above. The prey is a young sand martin which the hobby plucks and eats on the branch of a willow.

The falcon roosts in a tree-hole only metres away from the dormitory of swallows. As long as they keep coming, it will stay, but once the swallows have gone it will begin its own migration to Africa. Temperatures drop below zero during the night, and the reeds sparkle with ice. Insects are becoming scarcer now – most will spend the winter hidden away as dormant eggs, larvae or pupae. In the colder months only tiny gnats and flies will venture into the air so there is little food for swallows. These are potent signs that summer is degenerating into autumn, so now our swallow flies with fresh resolve as he leaves the roost at dawn.

After flying 120 kilometres he reaches Portland Bill, the very tip of a peninsula dangling into the English Channel. The autumn exodus is at its peak and huge numbers of swallows funnel down this finger of land, congregating in serried ranks along every telegraph wire. In this mass of restless birds our cock swallow loses contact with his family. Unlike swans and geese who must learn their migration routes from their parents, it isn't crucial for a family of swallows to travel together. Some do, but our cock bird must continue south with strangers. Because flying conditions are ideal, with perfect visibility and a slight cross-wind, there's an urgency to leave. Wave after wave of swallows stream out over the sea.

The Channel crossing is no ordeal for birds that fly as efficiently as these. Their long wings maximize lift and reduce drag, so they can travel farther and faster than rounded-winged warblers or finches on the same amount of fuel. In less than two hours the flock containing our cock swallow sweeps over the French coast. They hawk for insects over a reservoir before choosing a field of maize in which to spend the night.

The next day our swallow and a flock of thirty others head off through France. They don't fly in tight formation but stay well spaced out so that they can manoeuvre after insects without fear of collision. It's warm and sunny, so food is plentiful and the group makes good progress, travelling at altitudes between 50 and 100 metres. The birds follow a heading that takes them down the western side of the country.

High pressure brings clear skies day after day, so the swallows calculate their position using a sun compass. On its path across the sky from east to west, the sun moves 15 degrees in an hour. The swallows use an internal clock to keep tabs on this movement, and calculate their position accordingly. Of course, this system doesn't work when the sun is hidden from view.

For much of the route there are compact green fields and the odd château or village. But as they get near to the Mediterranean they encounter some very different landscapes. The swallows swoop over an immense sea of stones lying on top of bone-dry silt, a region known as Plaine de la Crau. There's not a single cloud to shield the sun, and this daunting landscape is a blinding white. The birds move on quickly, for there are few insects here. They come to Les Alpilles, a ridge composed of white rocks, weather-beaten into bizarre shapes, and dense thickets of prickly-leaved oaks, rock rose, juniper and aromatic herbs, which does provide in-flight food. Leaving this bizarre landscape behind, the swallows come to the

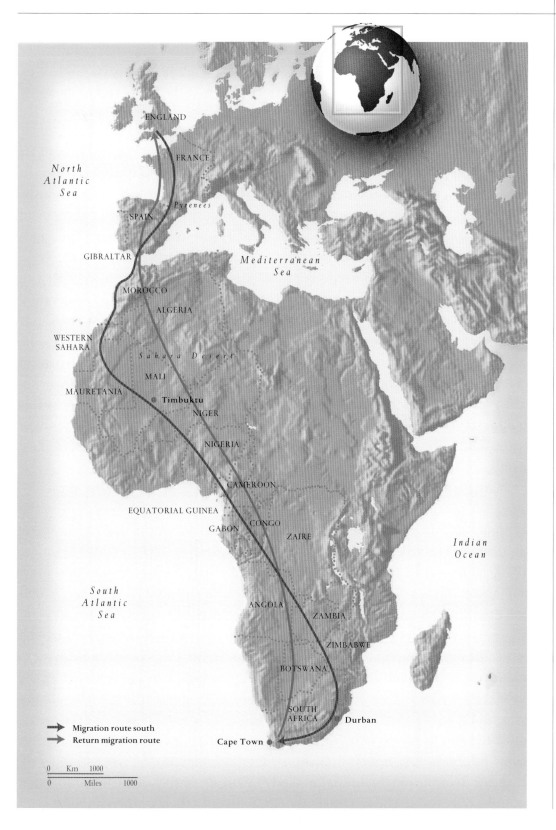

ENGLAND

FRANCE

North Atlantic Sea

Pyrenees

SPAIN

GIBRALTAR

Mediterranean Sea

MOROCCO

ALGERIA

WESTERN SAHARA

Sahara Desert

MALI

MAURETANIA

• Timbuktu

NIGER

NIGERIA

CAMEROON

EQUATORIAL GUINEA

GABON

CONGO

ZAIRE

Indian Ocean

South Atlantic Sea

ANGOLA

ZAMBIA

ZIMBABWE

BOTSWANA

SOUTH AFRICA

Durban

Cape Town •

→ Migration route south
→ Return migration route

0   Km   1000

0   Miles   1000

delta of the Rhône, the Camargue. This is a flat, windy land of marshes and brackish lakes, some with pink rafts of flamingos which seem to wobble because of the heat shimmer. There are wild white horses here too, which have the usual entourage of flies. These are snapped up by the swallow flock. The birds are beginning to sense that such food will soon be very hard to find.

The swallows have pressure sensors in their middle ears and they detect an approaching weather front. Soon the wind shifts direction and increases in strength. As it gets dark the stems on which they perch begin to sway ominously. In the early hours of the morning, our cock swallow has to grip tight to avoid being blown from the reeds. Daybreak reveals piles of billowing grey clouds heaped in the sky. The bad weather will delay the migratory flocks.

The cool temperatures keep insects deep in cover and the birds are forced to search hard for food, using techniques that our cock swallow has never used before. He hovers close to the flat white flower-heads of cow parsley to pick off tiny insects hidden amongst the florets. On a tributary of the mighty Rhône he does circuits through riverine forest, brushing close to leaves so he can snap up moths and flies disturbed by his wings. As a last resort he even lands on a sandy beach to collect flies attracted to the refuse on the strand line. He has short legs and his feet are small and weak – he's never done anything but perch with them before. Out of his element, he shuffles along the sand, fluttering his wings like a giant moth in order to assist his feeble walk.

By these desperate measures he maintains his fuel reserves. Up ahead there is more bad weather but it is better to the east and, before heading southwards, the swallows head inland in order to skirt around the storm. Out of the flock of thirty swallows that travelled together through France, only he and four others remain. The maelstrom killed a dozen and the meagre diet of the others means they must stall their journey south until they can stoke up on insects. The sun is still obscured by clouds, so the cock swallow relies on other navigation systems to find his way. He has inherited a magnetic compass, so he can sense the angle of the dip of the earth's magnetic field which varies with latitude. The swallow also has acute low-frequency hearing which allows him to hear sounds generated by the wind. Low-frequency or infra-sound patterns emanating from wind coursing over ocean surf and mountain ranges, sometimes over 1500 kilometres away, allow the bird to perceive the world as a vast landscape of sound. Because of this ability he knows that, not very far ahead, the way is barred.

After flying for eight hours, he and the other swallows cross the forested foothills that lead to the mighty Pyrenees. To overfly their peaks is impossible, as the loftiest rise over 3000 metres. The flock must find a route where they can traverse the range at the lowest possible altitude. The sky is azure blue, but if there is a change in the weather the mountains will be dangerous. Our cock swallow sees the others vanish behind a wall of rock. This is where the range is cut by the Organbiddexha Pass and by this route he passes through the Pyrenees and forges into Spain.

Now the swallow is two weeks into his journey, and the farm in Somerset, southern England, is over 1000 kilometres away. He's overtaken the winter which is inexorably moving northwards, and there are plenty of insects on which to feed. Even so, he doesn't stay for long in one place, continuing southwards past theme parks and tower blocks, olive groves and vineyards, castles and cathedrals.

In Spain he's never alone, and always travels in a flock with between 10 and 100 other swallows. In the province of Andalucia they're joined by another splendid migrant – the European bee-eater. These birds nest throughout the Mediterranean, but their winter quarters are in Africa. They're almost twice the size of a swallow, with dazzling feathers of chestnut, green, blue and yellow. As they sail through the air, their mellifluous call seems to match their buoyant flight. They're aerial hunters too, but they don't compete with swallows, preferring venomous wasps and bees. Bee-eaters usually launch themselves from a perch to catch their prey. Because of these stops and starts, they don't keep contact with the swallows for long. Both bee-eaters and swallows are heading for the tip of southern Spain.

The huge rock that is Gibraltar looms out of the western Mediterranean, a gigantic marker for the narrowest point between Europe and Africa. All types of bird pass by here to reach their wintering grounds. Black kites come in August, while early September brings vast flights of honey buzzards; short-toed and booted eagles come later that month. Streaming by throughout the autumn are millions of smaller birds – pipits, thrushes, warblers, martins and swallows.

Our cock swallow laps the island and skims close to a troop of the Rock's famous apes – in fact they are Barbary macaques, the only wild monkey in Europe. How they came to be here is unknown: they could either have been brought over by sailors from North Africa, or be a remnant of a species once common throughout Europe before the last Ice Age. The monkeys hardly register our swallow who flits past in seconds – the weather is fine but he can't dawdle here. The notorious Levanter is an easterly wind which can cloak Gibraltar in cloud and mist for days on end. If he gets caught up in that, the swallow will be grounded until the weather clears.

Our swallow's migration route
takes him over Gibraltar. The
Barbary macaques here are the
only wild monkeys in Europe,
and they have a tail so compact
that they appear tailless.

The vineyards of southern
Spain provide hunting grounds
for migrating barn swallows,
yielding a plentiful supply of
in-flight food.

The sea passage is short, and soon North Africa with its mosques and minarets unfolds before him. In a flock with twelve others he follows a flyline down the coast of Morocco. The swallows are unaware that they are now in the territory of predators that catch and kill two million migrant birds every year.

These hunters are Eleanora's falcons, majestic birds named after a Sardinian princess of the fourteenth century. They come in three colour phases. Three-quarters of the population are like a large version of a hobby with a mousy brown back, a buff breast streaked with black, and a similar white-cheeked, moustachioed head. Another form is just as well marked, except that its plumage is suffused with a deep smoky grey. The darkest phase is glossy black, although close up its feathers are faintly barred. Yellow legs and eye rings are standard in all Eleanora's falcons.

These birds are long-distance travellers too, spending the winter on the island of Madagascar and in coastal areas of Tanzania. In their wintering grounds, Eleanora's falcons feed mainly on flying insects; they only become a scourge of small birds when the time and place are right. This raptor breeds very late in the year – in fact later than other birds of the Palearctic (the region that includes Europe, all of Asia north of the Himalayan Tibetan mountains, North Africa and much of Saudi Arabia) – so its chicks hatch when 5000 million migrants are teeming out of Europe. Eleanora's falcons hatch their young on the islands and sea cliffs of the Mediterranean and the adjacent part of the Atlantic Ocean. Their nesting colonies are strategically positioned right in the path of the migrants and are strung along a band of only 6 degrees in latitude. Eleanora's falcons breed at precisely the right time and in exactly the right place to rear their chicks on the flesh of small birds.

Close to some rocky islets, the cock swallow hears the scream of a raptor carried on the wind. A rakish silhouette materializes from the spume where rocks change waves into spray and comes towards him like a dart. Two other falcons launch off from a ledge to take up the pursuit, but the swallow has wrap-around vision – the ability to see through 300 degrees without moving his head – and keeps track of all three pursuers. The whole group converge upon him. The first falcon lunges with its feet, but our swallow side-slips the lethal thrust. The second presses home the attack: its talons strafe one of the swallow's tail feathers, but he jinks to safety. The third falcon stoops from above, but the swallow accelerates away with a powerful swerving dash. Our cock swallow has an evasive manoeuvre equal to any tactic of attack. He has proved his fitness and strength. The falcons soon give up the pursuit to return to vantage perches where they can scan the sea for a more vulnerable target.

Eleanora's falcons make a successful catch in about seven out of ten pursuits. Group hunting is common, but they also hunt alone. Ninety different kinds of birds, including swallows, have been recorded as prey, although they feed mainly on shrikes and warblers. These are optimum targets because they are not such good fliers as swallows and they also migrate at night. At dawn, after a sea crossing, the migrants seek a landfall; when the exhausted birds are over the water there is nowhere for them to hide and the falcons pick them off with ease.

After his ordeal our cock swallow veers inland, heading to the south-east. Insects are plentiful in the scrubby fields of southern Morocco. He must make the most of these, for now it's important that he increases his body weight by one third. Ahead lies the most gruelling stage of the journey.

The Sahara blankets almost the entire northern third of Africa and is the greatest of deserts, comprising nearly 8 million square kilometres of sand, gravel and mountains. Migrating birds must cross it as swiftly as possible for there is little opportunity to stop and feed; it takes swallows two to three days. Traversing more than 1500 kilometres of barren, waterless land is hazardous for any bird, but of all the trans-Saharan migrants swallows are the most likely to die in the desert.

At the start of the long trek the cock swallow is with six others. At first they make steady progress, but then the wind begins. Before long, particles of sand move in tiny rivulets below the birds. As the storm worsens, scorching gusts throw sand high into the air. Battling against the wind the swallows reach a hamada, a flat-topped plateau strewn with loose stones amongst which they can shelter. The storm rages until evening and the birds have to bivouac for the night. At sunrise, only five of them can continue. As the others lift skyward, one female is so exhausted that she can barely open her eyes. Later in the day her body will be devoured by a scavenging dragon. This metre-long lizard – a desert monitor – uses its tongue to smell out the casualty of the storm.

For the first time on this epic journey, the cock swallow ascends to an altitude of 6000 metres. From this height his acute vision scans 100 kilometres or more. Below is a vast gravel plain, but to the south-east there's a tiny speck of green. He drops down in a graceful arc to join other swallows above an oasis. They plummet past the green leaves of date palms to skim the surface of a pool and drink on the wing. There are insects here too, attracted by the goats in a nearby settlement and the camel trains that often pass through. Our cock swallow spends the day resting and replenishing his fuel reserves which have run low during the storm.

As he crosses the Sahara in good weather, our swallow hugs the ground and snaps up any insects on his fly way.

The metre-long desert monitor feeds mainly on locusts and other large insects, but it will also catch small rodents and even swallows grounded by exhaustion.

There is perfect weather for the second half of the Sahara crossing, and the swallows drink again at a lake near Timbuktu. The pace of the journey becomes leisurely again when the desert gives way to the farms and forests of Central Africa. Three days later at dusk, above the foothills of the Mbe Mountains in south-east Nigeria, the cock swallow is with a mass of others. The birds perform together in a spectacular air show. Some arc across the rising moon, whilst a thousand more spiral lower and lower with whooshing wings and chittering calls. In the few minutes before dark, our cock swallow and a million others sweep into the tall grass to sleep. Rubbing wings in just one square metre are swallows from Italy, Britain and Germany. The roost contains birds from a total of fourteen European countries. Some stay here throughout the winter but for others, like our swallow, this is just a staging post on the journey southward. The birds gather here because the 5-metre-tall grass is so dense that it's impenetrable for most predators. But it is the full moon tomorrow, and their sense of security will prove to be false.

In the nearby village of Ebok Boje some strange paraphernalia is prepared during the day. Palm twigs are coated in a sticky resin made from local plants, gourds are gathered and long poles are cut to just the right length. In the evening, a procession of young boys and girls begins to climb through the cassava plantations to the grassland above. Each of them carries a pole at least three times their own height, with a gourd impaled at one end. Slung across from their shoulders is a quiver made from sewn banana leaves, filled with fifty or more of the sticky twigs.

Our cock swallow is 20 kilometres away, above a luxurious canopy of green stretching farther than the eye can see. Here he trawls through the air for food. His wide gape forms a large trap for flying insects, and around the base of his beak he has stiff feathers, like bristles, which help channel tiny flies and other insects right into his mouth. Soon he must continue southwards, but for now he's drawn back to where he roosted last night.

In clearings in the grassland, the children complete their ingenious traps. Into the gourds they insert ten to twenty sticky palm twigs arranged to radiate in every direction like the bristles in a chimneysweep's brush. The catchers now wait quietly until wings whoosh within range.

As the cock swallow descends to the roost there isn't any obvious danger, but as he skims over the top of the grass a glistening trap is thrust into the air. With a dextrous twist, our swallow just misses colliding with one of the shiny twigs and drops to safety in the grass. All around he can hear the alarm calls of stricken swallows ensnared on the glutinous twigs. The bird catchers grab them and throw them into hessian sacks. Because there's a full moon, the swallows can be caught long after sunset. It's not pitch-dark, so the birds will move if disturbed. Some of the children beat the grass to force the birds to fly up within range of the traps, but the beaters can't get everywhere as the roost is so immense and our cock swallow is not forced from his hiding place.

He rises with the sun and wheels higher and higher. In the village far below, swallows that were caught last night are tipped out from the sacks. Most are still alive when they are plucked and smoked. The birds are a valuable source of food in a protein-starved community and the chief doesn't want the roost to be wiped out completely, so the trapping season starts just before Christmas and is limited to two months. But even so, every year in the 'village of swallows' the migration of 100,000 birds comes to a premature end.

Our cock swallow's urge to migrate is still very strong, and a few days after leaving Nigeria he's in the heart of southern Africa. In this primeval landscape, rocks and tawny grass are splashed with sunlight and new animals lumber into sight. He hasn't seen elephants before, but soon he's flying less than a trunk's length away. Their huge feet stir up insects from the savannah in much the same way that horses' hooves did in the pastures of southern England. There are biting flies here too. He caught his first horsefly many months ago and thousands of kilometres to the north; now he snaps up tsetse flies from the back of a zebra.

The African plains also provide a new and nutritious category of insect. The towering monuments of sun-baked mud have no significance to the swallow, but at certain times they provide a bonanza for birds. After rain, tens of thousands of winged termites issue from the mounds, twirling into the air on a nuptial flight. A successful outcome means that a few mated females bury themselves into the rain-softened soil and found new colonies. Most of the others are sky sacrifices and end up in the stomachs of swallows, sparrows, storks, bee-eaters, flycatchers, falcons and kites.

Our bird is in a flock with other barn swallows as he cashes in on a termite swarm. But in South Africa in winter there are about a dozen other swallow species as well. Some are resident, while others migrate from the tropics to breed. How do these African birds cope with the influx of swallows and martins from Europe? There are, after all, estimated to be around 300 million barn swallows here alone.

All these aerial feeders share out the insects by foraging in different parcels of air space. For instance, house martins from Europe feed high in the sky, about

50 metres up. Brown-throated martins, and the resident mosque swallows, feed below them at 20 metres or so. Even closer to the ground, perhaps within 5 metres, there are South African cliff, lesser striped and grey-rumped swallows, with barn swallows representing the European contingent. Wire-tailed and white-throated swallows fly low as well, but specialize in hunting over water. Of course competition is also lessened by variations in size, bill shape and manoeuvrability, so each species gravitates towards particular types of insect.

Our swallow climbs away from this mosaic of dry grassland and woodland to overfly the lusher foothills further south. Here, at between 1500 and 2000 metres above sea level, he enters the territory of Africa's rarest swallows. In the morning sun the rolling grassy hills are wreathed in mist that shines a luminous gold. This happens so often here that the habitat is called mist belt grassland. Swooping over a ridge, our swallow sees a pair of dark birds materialize from the ground. As the sunlight catches their plumage, he sees it is glossy blue with purplish reflections. One of the birds is a male with elegant tail streamers which narrow into slender filaments. These blue swallows are hawking for insects with which to feed their three chicks. When their beaks are full the parent birds seem to plummet into the grassland, as their nest is underground attached to an overhang in a pothole. Blue swallows have been known to build 5 metres below ground level. Remarkably, their preferred nest site is the entrance to the burrow of a termite-eating aardvark, a mammal with coarse hair, a tubular snout and long ears superficially resembling a pig. After the breeding season, the blue swallow migrates north to Uganda, Western Kenya and north-eastern Zaïre. Even though it may rear two broods every year it is seriously endangered, and there are only 2000 pairs on the planet. As he leaves this fragment of mist belt grassland our swallow flies over the reason for its decline – most of the blue swallow's habitat is now smothered by plantations of pine and Australian wattle. Drastic conservation measures are needed now to protect this most attractive bird.

In just two weeks our swallow is at the tip of southern Africa. Table Mountain, serene and grand, today swathed in swirling white cloud, marks the

Around 100,000 swallows are trapped each year by the villagers of Ebok Boje in south-east Nigeria. Ensnared on the glutinous twigs of the chimneysweep-type brush, this bird will provide a valuable meal for a villager.

end of his migration. He has no precise destination on the wintering grounds, but won't go farther south than this. His internal clock terminates the urge to migrate, and for now his long-distance journey is over. He's battled through storms, escaped the clutching talons of predators and overcome some

of the world's toughest terrains. Strong and fit, he soars through the spacious skies of South Africa. For the next couple of months he'll lead a nomadic existence, his movements determined by patterns of weather and concentrations of food.

Even now, preparations for the return flight have begun. As he twists in a thermal, a primary feather from his wing spirals away in an immaculate sky. The moult has begun. This is a gradual process, because a swallow's survival depends upon aerodynamic efficiency. One by one, over the next three to four months, new feathers grow through to replace old ones that have been worn and abraded by months of flight.

Our cock swallow is also becoming an adult. After the moult the fresh feathers on his underparts will be paler than before, those on his upperparts a more glossy blue, while his tail feathers will be much longer. He must be well fed and healthy to grow a perfect set and it's the length of those blue and white streamers that will determine how successful he is at attracting a mate on the breeding grounds.

In Betty's Bay near Cape Town, our swallow feasts on a type of food that's unusual for a bird that eats nothing but insects. A rooikrans tree — a type of acacia — is bedecked with thousands of pods which twist and split open to expose shiny black seeds, each ringed with a fleshy band of red called the aril. Flying into the wind, our swallow hovers and snatches a seed which it then eats on the wing. The seed is indigestible, but the aril provides nourishment which is probably why swallows are attracted to this particular tree. Nobody knows how the phenomenon of seed-eating swallows began. The introduced rooikrans tree is only a recent addition to the South African flora. Unfortunately, wherever it grows it displaces the indigenous plants, and the swallows help its invidious spread by dispersing its seeds.

Plentiful rains to the north bring a flush of insects to Botswana, and this is where the cock swallow spends his last weeks in Africa. At night, he roosts in the dense reed-beds of the Boteti River with three million other swallows. This colossal number of birds draws in predators from land and sky. At dusk, every swallow flies a dangerous gauntlet. A bat hawk, a specialist in twilight hunting, cruises to and fro. It usually takes bats as they leave their daytime roosts, but it can turn its talons to birds returning to a night-time one. The bat hawk is joined by African hobbies and red-necked falcons, all of which pass through the cloud of swallows and snatch a meal in mid-air. Less aerobatic Gabar goshawks ambush from bushes, flying low to attack.

Other predators come in darkness. A black mamba slips unseen into the reeds. Fidgeting at just the wrong time, one swallow attracts the reptile's attention. The snake strikes and injects lethal venom in a fraction of a second. It holds on until its victim is paralysed, before disengaging its inwardly curved teeth and swallowing the bird whole. An African barn owl also drops in amid the assembled birds. It has more of an appetite than the mamba which is content with a swallow every three or four days; the owl may eat six in one night.

Swallows attract predators wherever they assemble in large numbers to roost, so why do they gather together at all? The answer is partly that it may be warmer inside a large roost, and the wind speed is lower. Most importantly, these gatherings probably have a social value and act as information centres. Our cock swallow learns about hard-to-find insect-rich locations by watching the behaviour of his roost-mates. These advantages make it worthwhile to sleep communally rather than alone. In any event, the vast majority of assembled swallows avoid the attention of visiting predators — it's mostly the sick, weak or inexperienced birds that are caught.

Away from the roost, our cock swallow gets uncomfortably near to the most surprising swallow-catcher of all. Absorbed with preening on a reed that bends over a shrivelling pool, he doesn't notice a massive yellow eye or the water moving below. He delicately teases a tail feather through the mandibles of his beak. Suddenly there is an eruption of mud, slime and amphibian. A giant bullfrog lunges towards him. As the frog's jaws snap shut, the swallow streaks to safety with only millimetres to spare. The amphibian, about the size of a dinner plate, falls back with an ignominious splash.

Africa has supported our swallow throughout the winter, but to breed he must go north. There's plenty of food here for him and millions of other wintering swallows, but there's not enough surplus for them to rear chicks as well. In late February the swallow feels a familiar restlessness: his internal clock is once again telling him it is time to travel. The return journey is much quicker than the outward one. Our cock swallow has gained experience in migration, and he's heading for a familiar destination — the place where he was born. He takes a more direct route than the flight line of autumn and pushes the pace. He covers as much as 300 kilometres in a day, and with favourable winds his airspeed can exceed 70 kilometres an hour. One swallow record-breaker flew from Johannesburg to Leninsk-Kuznetskiy in Russia, a distance of 12,000 kilometres, in

thirty-four days. Our swallow wasn't quite that fast – he takes fifty days to reach southern England.

In recent times, the English countryside below him has been through many changes. Some of them have meant that fewer swallows return in spring. Between 1970 and 1995 there has been a precipitous drop in the swallow population of half a million birds, cutting their numbers by a third. They're disappearing for many reasons. Some modern farm buildings are effectively 'birdproof', so there are fewer nest-sites. Intensive farming has homogenized the landscape as well. The undisturbed patches where grazing animals stir up insects are disappearing, ponds – a source of mud for swallows' nests – are being drained, and hedgerows which provide crucial sheltered areas for feeding in poor weather are being grubbed up. In the milking parlours and pastures other invisible causes probably have the biggest effect of all. There are new chemicals, harmless to livestock and humans, but extremely effective at killing pests. It's thought they

Table Mountain, the southern marker for the end of our swallow's migration, looms over Cape Town. Before his return journey to Europe, he joins a gathering of others of his kind (opposite).

may affect swallows directly, or simply get rid of too many flies. But some safe havens still exist and, as more and more people become aware of the problems, the decline of this popular bird may be halted.

Many farms in Somerset, southern England, have traditional buildings and livestock – just what our cock swallow needs. If a swallow has bred successfully before, it will usually return to the same nest-site. Most first-season birds return to the general area of their birthplace, not the exact site where they hatched. About one in a hundred is an exception to this rule, and our bird is one of these. By remembering the landmarks he'd learnt as a youngster he steers directly to the farm that has a barn with an antiquated plough.

It's early May and his parents and other adults are already breeding. With no time to waste, he finds an unoccupied rafter with an old nest already in place and begins repairs. He collects pellets of mud from the edge of a puddle and uses his beak as a trowel to replaster cracks and holes. Once the renovations are complete he circles the nest-site, shouting his short twittering song, just fifteen seconds long, over and over again. The display attracts a two-year-old female whose mate was a meal for a bat hawk in Africa. As she approaches our swallow swoops down to the nest, enticing her to land beside him. She sizes him up, paying particular attention to his tail, which he fans out to flaunt. It's thought that females prefer males with long symmetrical tails as it takes a lot of energy to grow this adornment, and a male with a perfect one must be in good condition and parasite-free. Both he and the nest are to her liking, and that night she roosts close to him, indicating that they will become a pair.

In another twenty days the first of a clutch of five eggs nestles in the white feathers lining the nest. Smooth and glossy with a white ground colour, speckled with rusty brown and lilac-grey spots, the egg is just like the one from which our cock swallow hatched only ten months before. The hen swallow will produce one egg a day, and start incubation in earnest when the last one is laid. Then the cock will be kept busy catching insects for his mate as well as for himself, and ultimately for his chicks.

In terms of evolutionary history, the migration of north European swallows can only be a fairly recent phenomenon – only 15,000 years ago their present-day breeding grounds lay under a permanent sheet of ice. As the ice retreated the birds' migration increased in distance and became riskier, but they continued taking a gamble with these twice-yearly journeys. By migrating, they leave the brutal winter weather and resulting shortage of insects for a warm and relatively safe environment. In spring, in the higher latitudes of the northern hemisphere, there are long hours of daylight and an abundance of food. Few insect-eating birds can survive here all year round, so there is a vacuum which summer migrants flood back to fill. It seems that the advantages for rearing young make the risks of migrating worth taking.

Our cock swallow flies up to perch on a wire where he cocks his head and spreads his wings to bask in the sun. He's fortunate – only one in three swallows survives long enough to breed. His skill as a traveller has ensured that he'll pass on his genes to the next generation. This maestro of migration may make this incredible journey from England to South Africa and back another ten times – swallows can live for eleven years! Each spring, with a pinpoint feat of navigation, he'll return to this same nest-site. Surely his journey is one of the wonders of the natural world.

Our caribou is part of the George River herd. At over 750,000 strong, it is the largest herd on the North American continent.

2

THE CARIBOU'S TREK

A COW CARIBOU (*Rangifer tarandus*) lives her life en masse and on the move. It's only when she's giving birth that she chooses to be alone and in one place. At this dangerous time she doesn't want to be jostled and distracted in a large herd. She can't run away from predators, so her best defence is to remain as inconspicuous as possible — merely another boulder on the vast Canadian tundra. On a rocky ridge one cow's labour is coming to an end. For thirty minutes her sides have heaved and her tail has lifted rhythmically. Now the contractions become more violent and she throws back her head. She fidgets uncontrollably, standing, then sitting, then rolling on to

43

her side. Finally, with a gargantuan effort, she rises and her new calf drops to the ground. The bundle of new life is 60 centimetres long and 5 kilograms in weight, barely the size of an Arctic hare. The calf, a female, glistens in the spring sunshine until the warm wind dries her fur. Most newborn deer have spotted coats, but caribou are plain brown (to blend into the sombre Arctic landscape) with creamy underparts. Up close the tiny creature has a prominent black muzzle and eye ring.

The calf is the newest member of the George River herd. At three-quarters of a million strong it's the largest caribou herd on the North American continent, and probably the largest in the world. Their territory encompasses much of northern Quebec and Labrador between Hudson Bay and the Atlantic coast of Newfoundland, and south to the 52nd parallel.

For now the calf is motionless, but soon she will begin her incredible journey. If she survives it will take her 9000 kilometres in a year – the longest trek of any land mammal on earth. Lying prone she's at her most vulnerable, and her mother licks and nuzzles her to encourage her to stand. Unravelling spindly limbs, the calf wobbles to her feet – only to collapse as her legs bow and give way. She rests before trying again. Her mother takes this opportunity to eat the after-birth, from which she'll obtain nutrients that stimulate the flow of milk. On the second attempt the calf, still only twenty minutes old, teeters upwards and stands long enough to suckle and draw in a draught of warm, nourishing milk. On this rich sustenance – 20 per cent fat – the calf will grow rapidly. She feels the caress of her mother's rough tongue cleaning away the last of the birth membranes. With that task completed the adult moves a few metres away, grunts softly and lowers and bobs her head. The newborn calf hears and sees her mother and totters towards her; these first steps are the first of millions.

Throughout the calf's life mobility means survival, and by the end of her first day she can outrun a man. Our calf doesn't remain the newest member of the herd for long. Winter conditions were good, so about 85 per cent of the herd's adult females carried calves that reached full term. Births are remarkably synchronous, most occurring over a period of just two weeks. It's 9 June, the peak in this particular year, so there are thousands of births in a day.

The calving grounds are well defined, only 1–2 per cent of the territory covered in a year, and traditional – the herd have used them as their nursery for generations. They're located on a high, barren plateau on the eastern side of the George River. It seems bleak and inhospitable, but the calves have the best chance of survival here and that's why expectant mothers converge on this spot every spring. The sodden ground is cloaked with creeping shrubs and hummocks of sedge. Here and there in this patchwork of dingy greens the gleaming white tassels of cottongrass flow in the wind. These are all typical plants of soaking soil. The surface water here has nowhere to go because a layer of permanently frozen ground below stops it percolating away. Surprisingly, this constant wetness helps to protect the caribou calves.

Wolves are breeding now as well, but they can't give birth where the caribou do. They need a secure den-site for their pups and their intricate burrows can only be dug in well-drained soils, preferably with tree roots to give structural support. The sodden tundra is useless for families of wolves, so by choosing areas such as these the caribou keep their calves out of the way of a major predator. The nursing grounds also give some protection from the worst of the weather. The land undulates and there is shelter in the dips between the rock-strewn ridges. Cold, windy weather is as lethal as a wolf to young calves.

The first few days are perilous for calves, even with these advantages. Nowhere is completely hunter-free and, while our young female suckles, three boulders and a lichen patch away a newborn bull calf takes his first faltering steps. Caribou have acute hearing and smell but their eyesight is poor, so neither of the mothers notices the huge shape launch away from a rocky bluff. The bird has wings which span 2 metres of air, the well-spaced primary feathers at their tips looking like so many fingers moving gently in the wind. As the golden eagle wheels and soars, sunlight plays on the feathers on its nape and lower back and they shine a luminous gold – the source of its name.

Although the eagle's body teeters in a gust of wind its head is rock-steady, the yellow eyes focusing on the shapes below. Our calf is safe nursing directly under her mother as the bird's huge shadow passes over them and races across the tundra. But the other newborn is still in the open. From an altitude of nearly 50 metres the eagle tilts up its wings and plummets perpendicularly down. The calf is struck in the middle of the back: the impact snaps his spine and he dies instantly. His mother barely has time to turn before the eagle struggles into the air. In another fifteen minutes the prey will be unceremoniously dumped atop the eagle's eyrie, a bulky bundle of sticks on a cliff ledge high above the George River. The two chicks in the nest will feed well while there are caribou calves to be caught. Crisis time for the eagles will come later, when this food isn't available. If it's a good year for lemmings and hares, both young could survive. If not, the older chick will kill and eat its weaker sibling.

It doesn't take long for calves to grow too large to be a meal for an eagle. The cottongrass meadows – another reason why the nursery grounds are where they

To camouflage them on the drab
tundra landscape, caribou calves
have unspotted coats. But when
the calving grounds are
blanketed with snow, the babies
are dangerously conspicuous.

For any caribou calf, movement
is the key to survival. At a day
old they can outrun a man, and
at slower speeds their gait is so
economical that even the tiniest
calf can cover 30 kilometres in
a day.

are – provide concentrated nutrients to enable the mothers to provide rich milk for their young. In less than two weeks our calf begins to nibble on succulent sedge tips, as well. She grows rapidly and at two and a half weeks of age has doubled her birth weight.

Our calf has been part of a nursery band of cows and calves since she was a day old. At first they didn't travel far, but at six days old she could cover more than 15 kilometres in a day. Caribou are rarely alone, and the calf soon familiarizes herself with the sights and sounds of the herd. Whenever they travel there is a clicking accompaniment, a noise produced when the long ankle tendons slide over the bones in the foot. A single caribou can be heard over 27 metres away, so countless legs on the move cause a considerable din. As well as this communal clicking there are other individual sounds. A calf recognizes the grunt of its mother, who is just as familiar with her offspring's bleat. The grunting and bawling of many cows and calves can make the herd a noisy place indeed. Our calf learns not to approach an adult caribou other than her mother. Other cows sniff her just as her mother would, but as soon as her scent tells them she's not their own they jump back or even strike out with their hooves.

To the north of the calving grounds the nursery band is joined by yearlings, barren females and a few males. The bulls with whom our calf comes into contact remain aloof and are always on the periphery of the herd. Most are immature animals two to three years old; the calf will cover many more kilometres before she sets eyes on the mature bulls which are now in the middle and eastern parts of the George River herd's range. The sexes segregate themselves in this way to share out the food supplies.

Our calf's band travels in a north-easterly direction, covering 30 kilometres or more every day as they meander over a liquid landscape. There's water every-where, and on days with intermittent sunshine cloud shadows whip away to reveal its extent. Lakes, pools, rivers and streams glisten as far as the eye can see.

The caribou flow effortlessly over this testing terrain. They have expandable feet which splay out on soft ground or snow, becoming almost round to support their weight, while spongy pads underneath provide traction. Unlike most other deer, they also have prominent dew claws. These hang above and behind the hooves proper, flaring out for extra support if a caribou begins to sink in gluti-nous mud or soft snow. These versatile feet are perfect paddles as well. Caribou are good swimmers, and they need to be – on the summer range, rarely a day goes by without a lake to cross or river to ford.

Early July is probably the most peaceful time of year for the caribou herd. Our calf, now nearly a month old, takes more solid food but is still being sustained by her mother's milk. The adult caribou spend over half of their time feeding on the fresh young leaves of sedges and shrubs, birch and willow. The travellers drift from one feeding ground to another. Every so often they stop and lie down to rest, chewing the cud just as cows do. To cope with a diet so high in fibre the leaves are first soaked and softened in a special chamber in the stomach, before being passed back into the mouth. At rest, the caribou work their jaws rhythmically to crush their food a second time around.

Under a vaulted sky of flawless blue the tundra is at its most pristine, and our calf leaves her mother to explore. A long-limbed lollop takes her along a beach of pure white sand where her movements are mimicked by another — her own reflection in a lake. A tiny bird runs alongside her and takes off into flickering flight. Its head and chest are jet-black and it has a glowing chestnut nape. The Lapland bunting's display flight takes it above the caribou herd, where it circles around before commencing a skimming glide. As it descends, its tinkling voice floats on the breeze. As the bird lands, its underparts catch the sun and our calf sees a flash of luminous white. The male bunting scurries off to snatch up some insects to take to his hen, who sits tight on a nest at the base of a willow, incubating a clutch of five eggs.

The calf clambers over a jumble of boulders, a reminder that it's not always a balmy 20 degrees centigrade like today — the pressure of winter's ice forced the boulders inexorably to the margin of the lake. On a gravel spit the calf inadvertently disturbs a bird much larger than the bunting. In a simple scrape on the ground, a semi-palmated plover sits on four eggs. A camouflage plumage of black and brown makes it difficult to distinguish bird from rock or sand, and if she continues along the same path our calf will trample the nest. The plover explodes away, stopping the young caribou dead in her tracks. Our calf watches as the bird puts on a frenzied display, running lopsidedly as she drags a wing along the ground. The bird feigns injury in this way primarily for the benefit of predators — pretending to be easily caught prey, she can dupe bears or Arctic foxes into following her. Remaining just out of reach, she'll make a miraculous recovery when she's led them away from her clutch. Once they've left her territory, she'll then return discreetly to incubate her eggs. Our caribou calf has no designs on plovers or their eggs, but the bird's evasive manoeuvre still has the required effect. The deer is distracted just long enough to notice a group of other calves and change course towards them. The indignant plover comes back to eggs that have not been crushed, shaken or stirred.

Many baby mammals play, but few are as exuberant as caribou calves. A small pool is the focus, and our calf and another of about the same age race round and round in dizzying circles. Every so often they reverse direction so that the chaser becomes the chased. On their spindly legs they circle so tightly and with such momentum that they seem about to spin right into the tundra. Sparkling like diamonds, a trail of water droplets ricochets off their hooves. The game ends with the grunts of their mothers – the herd is on the move again.

The playful calves are unaware that in the stagnant pool they disturbed creatures that will soon plague them. Tiny forms float back up to the surface when the caribou have left. Some are long and fragile, with segmented bodies and bulbous heads. They seem moustachioed, but these moustaches are in fact feeding brushes composed of a thousand or more bristles. To draw in a current of water and microscopic food towards their mouths, the mosquito larvae move the brushes like two hands simultaneously beckoning. The other forms in the pool are shorter and stockier in shape, like three-dimensional commas – these are the pupae of mosquitoes. Normally both stages hang suspended from the surface, but if there are shadows or vibrations such as those caused by the caribou calves they retreat to the bottom – disturbances of the water or a shading of the light could just as easily be caused by predatory birds or other enemies. The larvae wiggle away from potential danger by thrashing their bodies from side to side. Most insect pupae remain fixed in one spot but not those of mosquitoes: to submerge they tilt their bodies and flap their tails, which have a pair of paddles at the end.

Soon each pupa will crack open and a slender-legged flying adult will emerge. The stagnant water that collects in every low spot on the tundra is a productive hatchery, and in the warmth of the northern summer mosquito numbers grow and grow until the whole landscape whines. Male mosquitoes feed on nectar – it's the females that need a meal of blood in order to develop a batch of eggs. In mid-July the swarms become a debilitating scourge – observations show that on a man's exposed forearm the attack rate can be 298 bites per minute. From this it's been calculated that if a man was naked and standing still he could suffer 9000 bites per minute, and lose half his blood in less than two hours. The mosquito multitude means that the caribou never lie down – they stand, walk or run.

On a warm, still day the mosquitoes become intolerable. In a desperate attempt to escape the insect torment the caribou, with heads and tails held high,

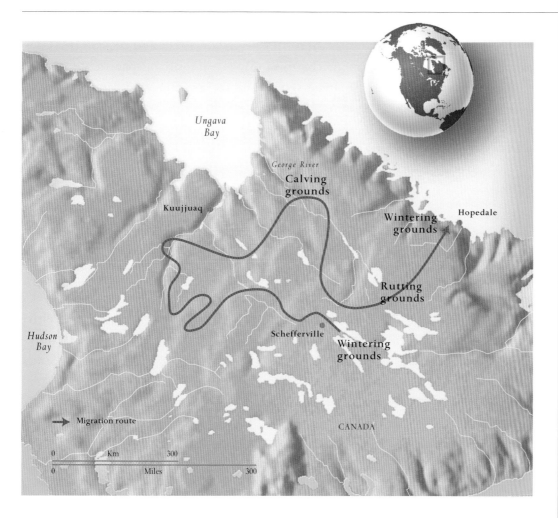

Ungava
Bay

George River
**Calving
grounds**

Kuujjuaq

**Wintering
grounds**

Hopedale

**Rutting
grounds**

Hudson
Bay

Schefferville

**Wintering
grounds**

→ Migration route

0   Km   300

0   Miles   300

CANADA

trot across the tundra at speeds of up to 50 kilometres an hour. The mosquitoes
are also the driving force for bigger and bigger herds. There's less chance of harass-
ment for each individual in a mass, so bands of caribou merge.

Our calf stays close to her mother as the travellers head for higher ground.
They reach an area that's bare and windy, with ridges delineated by gleaming ice
and scattered patches of stubborn summer snow. The wind whistling amongst
the rocks forces the weak-flying mosquitoes to drop to the ground, so the herd
can stop and forage in relative peace.

On a less blustery day the caribou crowd on to a snow patch where the lower
temperature keeps some of the mosquitoes away, but certainly not all. Thousands
still feed on our calf where her fur is at its thinnest, around her eyes, ears and
muzzle. She can hardly see, and she's lost 150 grams of blood. A stiff breeze is a
balm, and the calf orientates into the wind to dislodge some of the pests. When
the wind dies away she virtually has to run on the spot as the herd forms into a

compact milling circle. In desperation they begin to gallop, and the calf becomes part of a moving wall of caribou. The mosquitoes are easily outpaced, but for the panting caribou relief is short-lived. Their breaths are a beacon for the insects, which zig-zag along the carbon dioxide beam to feast on blood once more.

Constantly harassed, the caribou can only spend a third of their time feeding. It's the adult cows in particular which rapidly lose condition. Their reserves are already low from the rigours of calving, some of them weakened to such a degree that they'll be killed by predators or winter's cold later in the year. As our calf nuzzles for milk she feels how thin and tattered her mother has become. The young animal will soon be weaned, and rarely suckles now. The scruffy appearance of the adults is exaggerated by the moult: a new dark summer coat is showing through the worn-out winter pelage. Once luxuriant and silky grey, this winter coat is now threadbare and greyish white because of bleaching and breakage of the long hairs. Caribou tolerate temperature extremes of 30 degrees centigrade to 40 degrees below zero, so different summer and winter pelts are essential.

For just under a month the herd's sporadic movements through the uplands have been dictated by mosquitoes. Because of them, the caribou often travel farther each day than at any other time of year. Thousands of hooves etch their mark on the land, wearing away soil and even carving trails into rock. One afternoon in early August there is an immense aggregation of 100,000 caribou. They move at the same pace, crossing the undulating Quebec landscape with purposeful momentum. Small groups within the throng shift position, causing waves to be radiated outwards like ripples in a pool. As they reach the distant horizon the tightly packed herd resembles a giant carpet being dragged over the hills. Our calf is part of one of the earth's greatest wildlife spectacles.

The setting sun daubs the sky a brilliant orange as the great herd begins to disperse. Lines of caribou radiate across the land, and on every ridge animals are silhouetted against the sky. The caribou glow in the sun's dying rays and, like smoking chimneys, mosquitoes spiral above. There are fewer of these insects now, and their influence is declining, but in late summer other creatures come which literally terrify the caribou.

Imbibing nectar from tundra flowers are flies which seem harmless enough. Their appearance is magnificent – large and brightly patterned with tawny and black fur, they could be mistaken for bumble bees except that, like all flies, they have only a single pair of wings while bees have two sets. The breeding habits of these bot and warble flies are extraordinary and gruesome: their larvae feed on the flesh of living animals.

A bot fly perches on a pebble, poised and waiting for a caribou to pass. Walking next to her mother, our calf pays no attention when the fly launches its assault. One of the fastest flying insects known, the bot accelerates towards her face at a speed of 30 kilometres an hour. Its target is the calf's exposed upper lip. The cow caribou hears the fly's characteristic drone. She shudders and luckily knocks her calf out of the way as the parasite sprays its maggot brood into thin air instead of onto the calf's moist lip. The larvae fall to the ground, where they will soon desiccate and die. If they had been sprayed on to the nostrils or lip the maggots would have crawled along the roof of the mouth to feed and grow in the nasal passages. Heavily infested caribou can't breathe efficiently, which can be disastrous for a creature that relies on cardiovascular fitness to outpace predators.

Warble flies have a different tactic. They perch directly on the caribou's fur and extend a telescopic egg-laying tube to clamp and glue eggs on to the hairs of their host. Upon hatching, the larvae bore through the hide and feed on the muscle tissue within. Some caribou harbour thousands of these parasites. The short, fat, corrugated grubs have spines for extra grip and must cause considerable pain.

Parasitizing an animal that ranges over thousands of square kilometres of tundra means that these flies must make incredible journeys of their own. On the trek to the calving grounds in May, some nine months after they hatched, the mature larvae of both bots and warbles squirm out of their hosts and drop to the ground. Adults emerge in four to six weeks, but they're scattered along the route and must find the deer from a long distance away. To achieve this they have orientation skills and powers of endurance that are truly remarkable. To home in on their prey they detect the chemicals that emanate from caribou urine and the glands between their hooves. To catch up with the herds, these insects can fly non-stop for great distances. Warble flies can keep going for 400 kilometres, bots for 900, and both species can fly 250 kilometres in just ten hours.

After the bot fly's near miss, our calf and her mother flee. Running isn't very effective against these strong-flying and persistent parasites, but galloping away is the caribou's only option. Attacks by bots and warbles can cause panicked animals to stampede: the probable cause of the fragmentation of the huge summer herds.

During this terrible time our calf and her mother range widely with a small band of caribou, moving about 40 kilometres every day. They wander over a raw landscape, the legacy of the Ice Age 8-12,000 years ago. Huge areas of rock have only the sparsest covering of soil, as if the granite carcass of the land has been picked clean by scavenging wind and ice. Sometimes the calf has to struggle over immense boulder fields: these dark rocks were juggled by rivers in a glacier before

On expandable feet, which splay out on soft ground, caribou flow effortlessly over the water-logged tundra. They also have dew claws above their hooves which flare out for extra support.

A warble fly clambers on a caribou before extending its telescopic egg-laying tube to clamp and glue eggs onto the fur. When they hatch the larvae feed on the muscle tissue below the skin.

being dropped ignominiously where they remain to this day. As the caribou band drifts slowly and randomly away from the summer pastures, showers of snow become more frequent, but the cold brings an end to the flies. Most caribou, however, harbour grubs which will feed and grow inside them until the following summer.

It's mid-September, and for the caribou this is another golden time of year. The herd is at peace, as it was when our calf raced her reflection on the lake shore. Now, as then, insect numbers are low, so the deers' reserves aren't sapped by constant travel and fitful feeding. The herd wanders slowly over tundra which for once is colourful, even flamboyant. Frost has painted the land crimson, gold and scarlet by breaking down the pigments in the leaves. In ungrazed areas there are plenty of succulent grasses and sedges, and new foods too. Our calf learns about these by foraging close to her mother. There is a cornucopia of berries: raspberries and blueberries, curlew berries and cranberries, bunch-berries and bakeapple berries. The caribou sample these but don't gorge on them like bears. For these deer fungi are the real delicacies of autumn, and they avidly seek them out wherever they may grow. At last the caribou can put on fat for the challenge of winter, but before then the bulls must challenge each other in the rut.

At the end of September our calf is foraging next to a small stream when a shrub starts to shake. Startled, she backs off as a mature bull lifts his head – a truly imposing sight. Over the summer she herself has sprouted a pair of spikes, but these antlers are nothing when compared with the bull's. His are huge, over 1.5 metres in length; the wrist-thick main beams sweep back, up and forward before opening out into flattened palms. The palm of his left one has ten forward facing points, the right one only nine. All antlers of caribou bulls are extremely variable – it's rare for any pair ever to match exactly and no one caribou's antlers will be the same as another's. The lower part of the bull's headgear is just as impressive. Branching off at the base of the main antler beams are the brow tines, one of which is a simple prong, while the other expands to form a broad 'shovel' (so called because hunters thought it was used to shovel snow and uncover food, but its function is for protection) that projects forward over the muzzle. In some bulls the brow tines can be equal so that two large palms lie side by side over the forehead, but these double shovels are rare. The bez or second tines are the final part of the rack: arising just behind the brow tine, they swing laterally and forwards in a graceful arc, both parts becoming palmate at the tips.

Our calf watches as the bull continues to drive his antlers through the foliage of an alder which is already battered and frayed. The antlers are completely free of the skin or 'velvet' which covered them when they were growing. The colour of fine mahogany, their freshly polished surfaces gleam in the autumn sunshine. This thrashing of the vegetation isn't purely to enhance the antlers for aesthetic effect. The bull must get used to the feel of the elaborate weapons on his head, as well as strengthening the muscles in his neck. This season also brings pent up aggression which bush smashing helps to release.

Before long the mature bulls will have to fight, and the calf will witness these impressive antlers in action for the first time. As with every other aspect of the George River herd's life, the rut takes place on the hoof. Mock combats have been under way for a month or more, but the first real fight comes on a cold, grey day in mid-October. The six-year-old bull, which our calf saw tussling with the alder, sweeps through the herd grunting raucously. In preparation for the exertions of the rut his weight has increased by 20 per cent and his muscular neck is twice its normal size. Younger bulls turn down his challenge and run away. But this time he approaches a cow at the same moment as a veteran, two years his senior. Matched in size, the bulls spin towards each other. Striding along the same line they tilt their heads to show off the shape and size of their antlers. In this case their adornments are equal; symbolic posturing isn't enough and neither one will back down.

They become still and from a break in the clouds a single shaft of sunlight illuminates these magnificent animals as if in a spotlight on a stage. Their huge dark eyes are accentuated by a circle of short, light hair. The contrast between the flowing white mane on their necks and the rich, chocolate brown fur on their back and chest is made startling by the sun. They run at each other and the top points of their antlers smash together. The clatter of bone against bone frightens our calf, but this is just another sound of the herd – something she'll hear every October for as long as she lives. Stones and soil spin off the bulls' scrabbling hooves. With antlers enmeshed, they push and shove, twist and turn, each trying to force the other back. Panting furiously, they disengage before clashing again. During the lunge the points of the veteran scrape harmlessly across the shovel of the younger bull – without the protection of this shield across his snout, he could lose an eye. With lowered heads the bulls joust for five minutes, but the intensity of the fight is too much for the veteran. Pushed back down a slope he half falls, but he manages to turn and flee before he is gored. Fighting between equally matched males can result in injury or even death for the loser.

The victorious bull mates with the cow over which the dispute began, and he'll spend the next three weeks in a frenzy, relentlessly pursuing cows and fighting males that get too close. With his size and strength he's assured of many matings – about a dozen in all. To achieve them he'll need all his reserves, because during the rut he'll have no time to eat or rest.

The bull won't always run with the same cows. The females move freely between groups, leaving and joining at will. Our calf and her mother travel with the same bull for the duration of the rut, and at the end of October he approaches them. Both adults look magnificent with their newly moulted coats, although the cow doesn't have such a substantial mane and her antlers are small and spindly. They still bear shreds of velvet, as female caribou begin to grow antlers much later than the males – in July rather than in May. This is because antlers are crucial to the females in winter, not during the rut.

Antlers of caribou bulls, while growing, are covered with skin or velvet which the deer rub away when their antlers are hard and fully grown. Their headgear is covered in blood from the residual circulation beneath the velvet.

While he courts her mother, the bull pays no attention to our calf: she'll only attract the interest of males next autumn when she's sexually mature. The bull advances with his neck stretched forward and nose parallel to the ground. The cow would move off if she wasn't ready. To confirm that she's in oestrus, the bull sniffs her rump and urine. They mate when she is ready. He clambers on her back, but she stumbles and nearly falls – at 270 kilograms he's double her weight. Their union is swift and when it is over the bull loses interest immediately. Female caribou are mated once a year; other than the odd investigative sniff bulls will ignore our calf's mother for the rest of the breeding season.

In November the rut is at an end. Because of their contests to sire the new generation the big bulls have paid a high price They're more vulnerable to the stresses of winter, and this is one of the reasons that in most caribou herds cows outnumber bulls by a ratio of two or more to one. Some bulls have been injured and all are exhausted, with depleted supplies of fat, but the rut has a purpose. It ensures that the new generation is sired by the fittest bulls. By putting so much effort into fertilizing females some males may have lessened their chances of survival, but it's their best chance of leaving descendants to trudge into winter just as they themselves are doing now.

The autumn migration begins in earnest after the first heavy snowfall. The George River herd tramps southwards across a land shrouded in a freezing white blanket. Every year they spend 70 per cent of their time in snow, but they are the deer of the north and have many adaptations for conditions such as these. Our calf has a full winter coat: thick, hollow guard hairs to trap warm air protrude from dense woolly underfur. To prevent frostbite her muzzle is well furred right to her lips – most other deer have naked flesh around the nose. There has even been a change to her feet. In winter the pads underneath have shrunk and hardened and her hooves have grown to a remarkable degree. Their rims now bite into ice or crushed snow, protecting the fleshy pads from contact with the frozen ground.

She also has internal adaptations to conserve warmth. In her legs there is a counter-current circulatory system, which means that the veins returning blood from the limbs are very close to arteries carrying warm blood from the body. Much of the heat that would otherwise be lost is transferred from one to the other and returned to the body. This elegant design means that the temperature in the caribou's legs stays at 10 degrees centigrade or less, compared with the normal body temperature of 40 degrees centigrade. Cooler legs bring another advantage: they are in close contact with snow for much of the year, so if they were as warm as the rest of the body there could be a tremendous heat loss to the outside environment; but the tissues of the legs and hooves are specially adapted to function at these lower temperatures. The calf will certainly need these adaptations to withstand the next six months. Caribou are the only deer that can survive in constant snow and ice, with temperatures that can plummet to minus 50 degrees centigrade.

For now, however, the snow isn't too deep, and in early winter our calf and her mother cope well with the cold weather. They're in a small band of cows and young bulls. The winter range is so vast that the paths of most individuals will not cross again until the mosquito-induced aggregations of summer. The autumn rut is the only time when all age and sex groups unite. Caribou have no specific destination on the wintering grounds. Our calf's mother spent most of last winter near Sheafferville on the Quebec–Labrador border which is 500 kilometres away from where they are now.

The caribou's wanderings are dictated by food. The freezing conditions make most grasses, sedges, buds, leaves, berries and mushrooms unavailable. Now their staple diet consists of lichens, an amalgam of fungi and algae. Rich in calories and easily digestible, they're the perfect fuel for caribou in winter, although they contain few proteins and minerals for milk production and growth so the foods of summer are essential. Some sixty-two varieties of lichen are browsed by caribou. The type most commonly consumed is *Cladonia rangiferina* or reindeer moss. This 5-centimetre-high white, grey or green plant forms a miniature forest on the woodland floor; coincidentally its leathery, palmate branches are shaped just like the antlers of the caribou.

Our calf soon learns to locate lichens by smell, but she depends on her mother to uncover them and defend them against other hungry caribou. The cow kicks up showers of snow as she uses her versatile hooves as shovels. At the surface she makes long, pawing strokes but these become more frenzied as she digs deeper and has to chop away chunks of packed snow. The calf plays at digging by her side; she's too small to be much help, but gains experience in an activity on which, during life, she'll spend more time than any other. Sixty centimetres down there's a carpet of lichens, and the two caribou put their heads into the crater to feed. Before long they hear the tread of another caribou. It's a young male who's already dropped his antlers. This hard-dug lichen patch isn't extensive, and the cow prepares to defend it. As she lowers her head the bull backs off – lacking antlers, he is subordinate. The cow grunts and dashes forward to slam her head into his side. Winded, the bull exhales a spout of freezing air. Now she kicks out with her back leg and jabs her hoof into his side. Defeated, the bull moves off into the trees to dig a crater of his own. This is probably why caribou are the only species of deer in which the females possess antlers, and why cows keep their antlers long after the bulls have shed theirs. In this critical season they must be able to compete for scarce food resources, not only for themselves but also for the calf by their side and the one growing inside them.

In late December our calf is six months old. Far below the treeline she trudges through a woodland of birch and conifer. Protruding from the whiteness, the spindly treetops seem to be air-brushed onto the grey sky. Plump snowflakes descend languidly from swollen clouds, and for a second or so before melting they give the caribou spotted pelts. The herd now travel less than at any other time of year – following a recurring pattern of loops and circles, they cover only 5 kilometres in a day. It's milder now than of late, so rather than curling up to reduce heat loss while resting the calf stretches out languidly. In the early evening her mother digs a feeding crater in melting snow, but when they finish browsing the temperature plunges to minus 40 degrees centigrade. Because of the vacillating temperatures the woodlands will soon become inhospitable and the herd will be forced to move towards danger.

As our calf sleeps, the thawed snow refreezes to form an impenetrable icy crust. The next day it's impossible to dig down for lichens, but there's limited food high in the trees. The deer clamber onto deep drifts. These are usually avoided, but now they are strong enough to bear the weight of the herd. By using these frozen platforms they can reach the old man's beard, a type of lichen (not the climbing plant found in the hedgerows of Europe) that hangs from twigs in strands like candyfloss. But supplies are limited and the herd is forced to head for the Labrador coast, where the brutal winter is softened by the influence of the sea. After three days the caribou band find some hillsides where supplies of reindeer moss are plentiful. Now they can feed well, but close by there are creatures who have preyed on caribou for at least 25,000 years.

The migration route doesn't always bring the George River herd in close proximity to people, but this is an exceptional year and the caribou invasion is reported by the media around the world. At dawn it's quiet and peaceful in the community of Hopedale; the only sounds are clicking caribou tendons and hooves whispering on hard-packed snow. Our calf trots warily down the main street, a strange place with new and pungent smells of smoke and rubber, huskies and diesel. Other caribou weave amongst the wooden houses, shying away from the few windows that spill bright light into their path. The people who witness the spectacle know that caribou steaks will soon be plentiful.

The caribou band that includes our calf gather on the wooded slopes above the village. They're restless and will need a new feeding ground soon. The snow in this area has been turned over once, maybe twice, while they've been excavating food. The lichens below the frozen soil are protected by an icy crust that's difficult to dig through. In this way the caribou's method of foraging automatically prevents overgrazing and keeps them on the move.

The hunter comes in darkness when most of the herd are resting in a clearing. The sound of the skidoo is muffled by a belt of trees. A bitter blast of freezing wind dies away, to be replaced by a mechanical roar. Alarmed, the caribou stand and mill around. Astride his skidoo, the hunter is now only 50 metres away. As he breaks from the trees, our calf is dazzled by the light from the single headlamp.

To obtain lichens caribou spend much of the winter excavating craters in the snow with their hooves. In order to get at this food they sometimes have to dig as much as 90 centimetres down.

The man relies on the caribou not to flee immediately, although he's not sure what they'll do as he's never hunted at night before. When alarmed during the day the deer, known for their so-called curiosity, seldom run far before stopping to look over their shoulders. They may even circle and pass downwind and close to the threat, as if to confirm its identity by scent. This curiosity leads to many caribou deaths.

But at night there is no indecision, and the herd bolt away. As they run disembodied yellow spheres bob in the darkness. Like cats, the backs of their eyes have a built in reflective tapetum to concentrate light. This acts like a mirror and reflects the light from the headlamp back to the hunter. Unprepared for their rapid retreat, he only has time to fire once. Just ahead of our calf a victim falls: the young bull thrashes on the ground as if under the influence of an invisible puppeteer. As winter conditions have brought the George River herd close to people this year, the bull is just one of 30,000 that will be shot.

In some years the caribou walk right into the village of Hopedale on the Labrador coast. It's easy to shoot them from skidoos and the villagers will feast on caribou steaks and burgers.

The rest of the herd explode from the woodland to regroup on a treeless plateau where the frightened animals form part of a weird tableau. The only sound comes from lungs punching breath into the cold air. Behind the herd, the night sky is replaced by a changing palette of lurid greens, reds and yellows, swirling eerily. The Northern Lights are the result of electrical discharges among rarefied gases high in the atmosphere, a phenomenon linked to the earth's magnetism and most pronounced over the magnetic poles. The caribou soon forget their fear and some even lie down; tomorrow they will head west to find a new feeding area.

There are many herds of caribou across a great swathe of the circumpolar lands. For many northern peoples these deer are crucial. In Europe, the Lapps couldn't survive without them. In North America, the Tinne tribe rely on these deer to such a degree that they are known as caribou eaters. A carcass has a multiplicity of uses, as well as providing meat. The fat stored in the back becomes a carbohydrate-rich accompaniment to the lean steaks. A vegetable side dish is perhaps the most surprising of all: if taken straight from a caribou's stomach where they've been fermented with saliva and digestive juices for a while, lichens that are normally indigestible to humans become a salad called nerrooks. Fish hooks are made from the antlers, knives from the shinbone and a strong thread from the tendons. The hides provide clothing and insulation for dwellings.

Even though they belong to the same species, caribou in Europe and Asia are called reindeer. There are minor differences in appearance – for example, caribou have larger antlers – but a great difference in their spirit. Reindeer can be semi-domesticated and have been for centuries, the earliest reference coming from Chinese writings in AD 499. The Lapps in Scandinavia and some of the peoples of northern Russia wander with their reindeer herds between the summer pastures and wintering grounds. The animals move along routes that they followed when they were truly wild, but now the herders make sure that the females aren't disturbed on the breeding grounds and that most predators are kept at bay. But for the reindeer there is a price to be paid: their milk, which is 20 per cent fat, is made into cheese, butter and yoghurt and in October or November some of the reindeer are slaughtered for their meat. It is eaten fresh, smoked or dried and its flavour is said to be a hybrid between beef and mutton.

These animals have even been translocated to new territories, so successful is their partnership with people. There are tame herds in Greenland, Iceland, Alaska and Scotland, and they've even made the southern hemisphere. Before the First World War, reindeer were introduced to South Georgia for fresh meat on the hoof, and they are still thriving today. Caribou, by comparison, are always aloof, and all attempts to herd them have been singularly unsuccessful. When they migrate they must do so without people smoothing the way, but they are eaten just the same.

As she shelters during a blizzard, our calf is indifferent to the reindeer's way of life. She lies in the lee of a snowdrift where there is some protection from the stinging ice particles whipped up by the wind. The sky is full of spinning snowflakes and the calf can barely make out her mother, even though she is only a metre away. When at last the blizzard is over she follows the cow to feed. The herd have based themselves around a cluster of frozen lakes, fringed by forest. At first the forage is adequate: at the lake margins there are even horsetails covered by only a thin blanket of snow, but these are soon grazed. Really deep snow begins to encroach on prime feeding areas and makes the abundant woodland lichens inaccessible.

The caribou must forage on the poorer ranges on the slopes. To endure this poor nutrition, changes take place within their bodies. Their basal metabolic rate drops by 25 per cent or more, and growth ceases until spring. Even with these adjustments, daily activity expends more energy than is produced through the food consumed, and our calf's weight declines by 10 per cent. To obtain enough food just to survive, her mother spends over twelve hours a day digging more than 100 craters. Now the calf is totally dependent upon her mother to uncover food. The fuel reserves in her small body are stretched to the limit, and she must conserve energy wherever she can. Rather than pawing away snow herself, as she did in early winter, she waits patiently while her mother digs. In this desperate time skirmishes for ownership of craters are common, but as our calf's mother is high in the order of dominance she rarely gives feeding rights away – in fact, she often forces younger, weaker caribou to leave holes they've dug themselves. Our calf shares her success; she couldn't compete for food on her own. Mostly she grazes next to her mother, but today she's so hungry she attempts to push her away. Remarkably, she succeeds and the cow leaves the crater for her offspring.

As she lowers her head to graze, the calf is startled by a snow patch that seems to float into the air. As it turns, she sees it is a bird with pure white plumage except for slaty brown spots on its crown and back. Its huge yellow eyes are like searchlights. This is a male snowy owl – a female would have heavy dark brown bars, making her a much darker bird. The owl is as well adapted to the cold as the caribou – his feet are well feathered to the tips of his toes, and warm feathers also cover his bill; only his eyes are exposed. Snowy owls are Arctic specialists and have

The snowy owl shares the caribou's winter range and is a truly Arctic bird that can withstand temperatures of 60 degrees below zero. This is a young male owl — a female would have browner plumage.

The pelt of wolves can be any permutation of grey, black or brown. In winter many packs rely on hunting caribou to survive. The young wolves learn the ettiquette and technique of tackling large prey from the adults.

been found at the northernmost limits of the landmass, even in winter. They can withstand temperatures lower than minus 62.5 degrees centigrade, the lowest ever recorded in the northern hemisphere. In a laboratory experiment lasting five hours, one individual coped well at minus 93 degrees centigrade.

This snowy owl glides low past our calf before hovering and staring at the snow. Then he drops down as silent as a snowflake. Breaking through the frozen crust, he caves in a run in the snow and plucks out the occupant. The owl swallows the lemming in a single gulp. To maintain his body weight at temperatures such as these, minus 30 degrees centigrade, the owl needs four to six large lemmings a day. This is his seventh, so now he can roost. With eyes blazing, he takes off on a trajectory towards the trees. The great bird flies close to other impressive predators which possess eyes of marigold yellow. Six pairs now stare at the caribou, only 30 metres away.

The animals at the forest edge seem to be coloured in every permutation of grey. The wolf pack is led by its two founder members, known as the alpha pair. A subordinate female was shot earlier in the winter, but four young born in the spring remain. At just under a year old, the juvenile wolves are nearly as powerful as their parents. When the caribou herds first arrived on the wintering grounds, only the adult wolves were effective at bringing down prey, but because of the importance of training muscle, sinew and bone, and the value of learning the tactics of the hunt, the youngsters were present at every kill. With this experience and training they have become a formidable attacking force in their own right.

The caribou band drifts slowly towards the trees. The wolves' shallow breath vaporizes into delicate clouds, but it isn't this that gives them away. A strengthening wind carries the scent of the pack to our calf, who lifts her head and bleats in alarm. The wolves explode from cover in an instant. In a mêlée of thundering hooves and scuffed snow, the caribou head downslope. They aim for a frozen lake – running away from cover is their best chance of escape. In the open they can see danger clearly, and their fleetness of foot means they can outrun the pack. The wolves predict the caribou's course and cut the corner to intercept them. They excel in manoeuvrability and must force a situation which compromises the caribou's superior speed on the flat. Most of the caribou leave the lake shore and race away over the wind-packed snow and ice.

The wolves know that the deer, which have a firm footing and no obstacles in their path, can outrun them easily. They concentrate on the stragglers, accelerating straight into the path of eight caribou, including our calf and her mother. The group veers away and gallops towards a belt of pines. Forced to plough through a drift of energy-sapping snow, the caribou slow down. Amongst the trees and on soft snow, the agile and lightweight wolves have the advantage. Our calf sees the grey blurs streaking towards her. She flounders in a deep drift but, tenacious and strong, she keeps up with the rest. As the caribou turn towards the lake, the wolves cut the corner once more. An old caribou cow falls behind – the predators are watching for any sign of weakness like this. A juvenile wolf spurts into the gap between the old cow and the other fleeing deer. Looking back, lungs screaming for air, our calf sees the carnivore careen into the exhausted cow and slash at her shoulder. As our calf and her mother break from the trees, they bunch up with other caribou to confuse their pursuers – but there is no need. Behind them the wolves have doubled back: the chase is over. Weakened by repeated bites, the old caribou is finally suffocated when a juvenile wolf clamps his jaws around her throat.

As our calf trots back to the main herd, the wolf pack feasts on the kill. The alpha male gorges on the deer's fat-rich tongue. To get at the liver and internal organs, the other pack members slash and nibble away right inside the carcass. In winter these carnivores need more than 2 kilograms of meat a day. After the pack have polished off the flesh, they use their powerful jaws to fracture the long bones for the nutritious marrow they contain. In just three days all that remains are the hooves, the antlers, the stomach containing the last lichen meal, and a few scraps of hide and bone. The old cow was just one of many of the casualties of winter. In this season each wolf pack needs to kill every four to five days, and to tide them over the wolves of the north rely almost entirely on caribou.

Other deer were shot and even more died without the intervention of predators. They failed to accrue enough fat reserves during summer and autumn, so winter's brutality killed them outright.

Even so, the wintering grounds aren't littered with carcasses – they're tidied up by scavenging lynx, foxes and bobcats. One bird in particular is rarely absent at a carcass. Glossy black ravens are always ready to manoeuvre on mortality, pilfering gory titbits.

In March one of these sleek birds gathers something from the snow as our calf wanders past. This time the raven isn't feeding – her behaviour is a sign of spring. The bird's beak is crammed with caribou hair to use as lining in her nest.

The caribou sense this change in season as well: soon they must start the long march to the calving grounds. Our calf and her mother look gaunt – the

OVERLEAF: When swimming, caribou use their flattened hooves as paddles. Their luxuriant coats act as lifejackets which is why they ride so high in the water when they ford tumultuous rivers during the spring ice melt.

outline of their ribs can be seen through their coats – but they've survived one of nature's greatest ordeals. The restless caribou form into groups as the days lengthen, and changes in snow cover, bringing good walking conditions, seem to be the final stimulus to go. Our mother and calf join a band that is one of the first to leave. Heading northwards, the travellers choose paths of least resistance – windswept ridges, frozen lakes and rivers, shallow or crusted snow. They tread in each other's tracks; it's exhausting being the trail-breaker so the lead constantly changes. Sometimes our calf is right at the front – she's three-quarters of the size of the adult cows now, and hasn't the burden of a new life within.

With each passing day more of the George River herd's cows begin their journey. The constant flow packs down the snow, so that behind our calf's group paths are becoming tracks and tracks becoming trails. The caribou cows that leave later can have an easier passage on snow packed hard by earlier hooves, but with less time in hand if they're held up by snowstorms or intense cold they can end up racing to reach the breeding grounds, sometimes covering 65 kilometres a day, before their calves are born. Soon only the bulls who won't begin their trek for a good month and a half are left on the breeding grounds. By then decreased snow depths will make travelling conditions much easier for them and there will be nutritious new growth on which they can browse. Their journey doesn't have to be as arduous as that of the cows, who are driven by the need to reach a safe birthing place.

In early May our calf's band is far to the north, just leaving the zone of lichen woodland for the upland tundra. Travelling at 4 kilometres an hour, the caribou expend so little energy per unit of body weight that they are the most efficient travellers of any land mammal. With their economic gait they devour the tundra. It's only recently been shown that the routes which caribou follow are not determined simply by snow conditions: precise navigation, probably using a magnetic and sun compass, is involved, and the George River herd don't deviate from their narrow migration corridor by more than 15 degrees. They will keep on this bearing at almost any cost.

Our calf is nearing the end of her round trip, but there is still a formidable barrier to overcome. It can be heard before it can be seen – a cacophony of ear-splitting creaks, crashes and rumbles. This year the caribou have arrived on the George River as the ice is breaking up. The herd gather on the banks as ahead of them frozen blocks and chunks in all shapes and sizes surge and tumble together. Some ride up over smaller fragments as if they're a monstrous creature trying to climb from the water. There's a splintering sound as a pine tree is gouged from the bank and crushed between two ice blocks each weighing over a tonne. The caribou would rather die than fail to reach their destination: they must make this perilous crossing.

There's an ice jam upstream and the George River becomes quiet and still. Open water can be seen – an opportunity for the first caribou to plunge in, which encourages others to follow. Pushed by animals further back, our calf and her mother leap into the freezing water. At first the heads and backs of the herd form a continuous raft. They swim well, using their flattened hooves as paddles. Their luxuriant winter pelts provide buoyant lifejackets so that their bodies ride remarkably high in the water, with one third above the surface. Six kilometres per hour is their normal swimming speed, but in these treacherous waters they swim at 10. There is an ominous roar. The pressure of water breaches the ice jam and chunks of ice are hurled downriver with explosive force.

The herd stretches between both banks, and the brown raft of swimming animals is torn asunder by rearing ice blocks. Our calf puts on a spurt as an anvil-shaped block bears down on her. It clips her shoulder and knocks her under. The swollen river pushes her downstream, but her frantic struggles bob her back to the surface as behind them the ice block sails by. Her mother draws alongside. A gap opens up ahead and they swim furiously. Reaching the bank, they scramble to safety leaving the bodies of over 100 caribou to float downstream with the ice that killed them. Some were crushed like the pine tree, others were drowned.

The next morning the surviving travellers have come full circle. They stand on a windswept ridge where the only breaks in the sombre landscape are the brilliant white tassels of cottongrass flowing in the wind. For them this is a special place, and they have endured incredible hardship to be here. Soon the heavily pregnant cows will devote all of their time to a new generation. Our calf is one of the few yearlings that remain – most of the others dropped back in the latter stages of the migration. The yearling males were the first to leave; females stay with their mothers longer so as to learn the route to the calving grounds. Our calf must now make way for the new one and, when she approaches, her mother chases her away. The bond that kept them close until now is broken.

Our calf joins other yearlings on the periphery of the area occupied by the pregnant cows. Totally independent, she browses on the nutritious new growth along a line of snow melt. At just under a year old, she's walked 9000 kilometres and completed a truly incredible journey. She must never let up on this rhythm of travel if she is to find food and keep one step ahead of predators. Next spring she may have a calf of her own, and another life of movement will begin.

Pencil-sized young eels or elvers mass in estuaries before entering fresh water and heading up river.

3

THE
EEL'S
MARATHON

I N THE DARK ABYSS, 300 metres below the surface of the Pacific Ocean, sinuous forms twist and writhe. The creatures are silvery in colour, with huge bulging eyes and capacious mouths, although they haven't eaten for months. This dark and forbidding world is their mating ground, and several males assemble around the much larger female. They rub against her, gyrating slowly, sometimes bumping her swollen body with their heads. Suddenly the males become frenzied as the female begins to discharge millions of tiny spherical eggs. To fertilize them her suitors twitch and produce sperm. The spawning forms a cloud in the water through which the creatures pass as they swim slowly away to die. These short-finned eels (*Anguilla australis*) breed only once in a lifetime. Millions travel here to spawn, and the sea bed will be strewn with their spent bodies. The number of eggs they leave floating in the Coral Sea, an area of the Pacific west of the islands of New Caledonia, is beyond calculation. When they hatch, the progeny will attempt to reach the rivers of south-east Australia. Only a tiny proportion will complete this incredible journey of over 3000 kilometres. The young will spend years in fresh water before making the return trip to their birthplace to spawn and die themselves.

The short-finned eel is one of sixteen species of freshwater eels, so called because, even though they don't spend their whole lives there, they are the only members of the eel family who spend time in fresh water.

The adults are all similar in form, more a tube than a fish, with a mosaic of small scales deeply embedded in the thick, leathery skin. They have no pelvic fins and their other fins are united to form a single continuous fin along the back, around the tail and along the belly. They are widespread in countries that border the North Atlantic (Europe and North America have one species each) and western Pacific Oceans, from Japan through South-East Asia and the Pacific Islands to Australia (which has four species in all) and New Zealand, then westwards through the Indian Ocean to Madagascar and East Africa.

All freshwater eels start out as tiny eggs a mere 1.2 millimetres in diameter. Pacific currents as gentle as a breeze on the land soon disperse the short-fins' freshly spawned eggs. We travel with one egg as it revolves through the depths, and its cells begin to divide. Thirty hours after spawning, black shapes become visible through the egg's transparent casing: these are the heart and eyes. In another ten hours a female eel larva, 4 millimetres long and tadpole-shaped, is hatched. It has a yolk sac at first, but the nutriment which this contains is needed for the growth of fins, the opening up of a mouth and anus and the development of the brain, so by the seventh day the yolk has all been absorbed.

Hanging head down, the larva is still a passive drifter, but at eight days it can just about swim. The most striking transformations can now be seen on its head: the eyes blacken with pigment and the larva grows teeth which are truly bizarre. Gradually, one after another, these lengthen until the upper jaw contains one long grasping tooth and three smaller pairs. The lower jaw has four pairs of sharp same-sized teeth. This strange dentition gives our eel larva, still only 7 millimetres long, a sinister appearance. As it grows over the next few weeks, it flattens into the shape of a willow leaf and its teeth become smaller. At this stage the transparent larval eel is still quite unlike an adult and is called a leptocephalus. This strange apparition baffled early scientists and was a stumbling block in the unravelling of a puzzle.

The journey of the larvae to reach fresh water is as mysterious as it is incredible. To scientists, the life cycle of eels is a perplexing challenge. It took until the end of the nineteenth century to gain even an impression of these creatures' remarkable story, and even today the finer details are still to be resolved. Eels have been a gastronomic delight for centuries, but unlike other freshwater fish the millions that were caught and gutted contained no eggs and sperm. So where did baby eels come from? In ancient Greece, Aristotle was certain that they were generated from 'the entrails of the earth'. Pliny proposed they grew from fragments of the adult's skin. Others imagined that the hairs from a horse's tail could animate into young eels, or that a certain kind of small beetle gave birth to whole litters of them.

These fanciful notions were laid to rest in 1897 when a European eel caught in the Mediterranean was discovered to be a sexually mature female. This, combined with the observation that small eels appear on the coast, seemed to show that eels lay their eggs in the sea. But why were no eels smaller than 15 centimetres ever caught, and where exactly were the eggs laid? A transparent, leaf-like fish had been described in 1767, but it wasn't recognized as an eel; it was thought to be a distinct species of fish and was named *Leptocephalus brevirostris*.

The transparent fish's real identity was revealed 133 years later when a pair of leptocephali caught near the coast metamorphosed into young European eels. In 1904, now that this piece of the jigsaw was in place, Johannes Schmidt, a Danish scientist, began following a trail to the breeding grounds: the trail he followed was the eel larvae themselves. To collect leptocephali, he towed nets across the ocean, recording the dimensions of his catch as well as the time and place of capture. The journey of the larvae was mapped by following their decreasing size. The newly hatched, smallest individuals were found in a region in the south-west of the North Atlantic known as the Sargasso Sea and nowhere else, indicating that this was the spawning ground of the European eel. By extrapolation from Schmidt's findings and by subsequent drift net sampling in different parts of the world, it is theorized that all sixteen kinds of freshwater eels breed in deep warm waters. But to this day no mature eels have ever been caught away from the continental shelf.

Recently eels have been given hormone injections to make them mature and spawn in laboratory tanks. Under these artificial conditions observations have been made on courtship and the development of eggs and larvae, although unfortunately the young eels only survive for about fourteen days after hatching. Larger leptocephali can be fished for and then maintained in aquaria, but they still keep some aspects of their lives a secret.

For instance, scientists can only theorize about the purpose of such an obvious feature as the formidable teeth possessed by the young larvae. It used to be thought that eel larvae didn't feed at all, or merely absorbed nutrients through their skins, until they reached fresh water. The teeth were explained as being purely a calcium store, in readiness for the cataclysmic transformation of the leptocephali when they reach the coast. Then careful examination of leptocephali trawled from the sea showed that their simple guts contained an unidentifiable mush. In 1995 in Dr Hiro Kagawa's laboratory in Japan, eel larvae were seen bending to snap up rotifers (microscopic creatures) – the first report of such behaviour. This and other evidence suggest that in the open ocean leptocephali do use their teeth for feeding. Could they bite off chunks from gelatinous creatures or maybe impale tiny crustaceans? Nobody will know for sure until the larvae are observed in the wild. All these gaps in our knowledge mean that eel larvae remain enigmatic, and with regard to some aspects of their oceanic odyssey an educated guess is the best we can do. One thing is for sure: this is a perilous journey and with each passing day some of the millions that hatched will be eaten or otherwise perish.

With its strong teeth, an eel larva looks so unlike an adult that when first discovered it was thought to be a unique species of fish. When it reaches coastal waters the larva will transform into a recognizable miniature eel.

Our leptocephalus, now a month old, is a passenger on the East Australia current, more than 150 kilometres south of where she hatched. It's likely that she's not simply a passive drifter but actively swims to make vertical migrations (predominantly in the first 300 metres) – perhaps every day to the surface waters and back. She is part of the plankton, an enormously varied community of minute plant and animal organisms that is carried along in moving waters. In the open ocean there is nowhere to hide, so, like the eel larvae, many of these creatures achieve a high degree of invisibility by being nearly transparent.

Other than the insects, nearly every major animal group or phylum is represented here – in fact two groups, comb jellies and arrow worms, are found nowhere else but in the marine plankton. A swarm of comb jellies propel themselves past our leptocephalus by rhythmically beating tiny hair-like cilia which are arranged along their bodies in eight discrete bands.

The comb jellies look exquisite as they spin slowly near the surface: their bands of cilia catch and refract the light, so that wave after wave of shimmering rainbow colours sweep in lines down their transparent bodies. This particular kind is the shape and size of a

Comb jellies row through the water with eight bands of tiny hairs or cilia which refract light into shimmering rainbow colours. They are active hunters which lasso prey with a pair of adhesive tentacles.

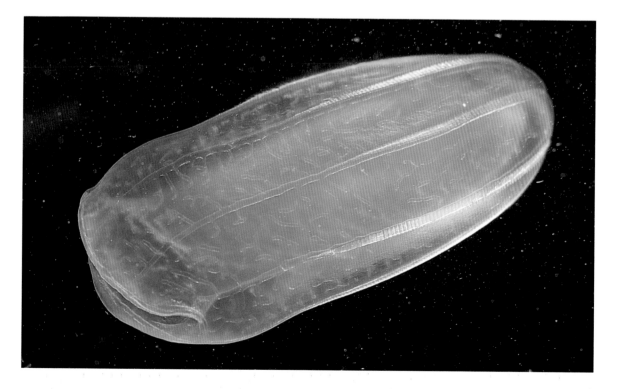

gooseberry. On the edge of the comb jelly swarm, however, there is a creature swift enough to be lethal. The sinister phantom waiting for prey is an arrow worm. It is shaped like an arrow with vicious curved spines on each side of its head. Our eel larva wriggles to avoid colliding with a comb jelly. With fins along the edge of its body, the arrow worm turns. It manoeuvres precisely. The leptocephalus is now only 2 centimetres away, and if she moves she'll be hooked. The arrow worm detects the ripples of its prey. With an up and down flick of its tail the deadly hunter darts forward like a torpedo. It brushes close to our eel larva and seizes a copepod crustacean. Our leptocephalus escapes because the copepod twitched – and for a striking arrow worm a moving object provides a much stronger stimulus than a stationary one.

As she floats through the upper layers of the sea, the eel larva passes by many other glories of the plankton world. The most common varieties of salps, floating sea squirts, are shaped like open-ended kegs. To propel themselves through the sea they pulse rhythmically, to pump water into the opening at the front and then out of the back. Some species form into colonies – hundreds or thousands join together in a convoluted chain. Individuals work in unison so that the jet-propelled salp streamer functions as a single organism as it swerves around our leptocephalus. Salps are the cows of the sea, filtering microscopic plants from sea water.

Tentacles laden with explosive stinging cells trail right across the eel larva's route. The longest traps belong to the siphonophores, a group which includes the Portuguese man o' war. They behave much like a single animal, but they are composite creatures consisting of a thousand or more varied individuals. Some are responsible for defence or for capturing prey, while others specialize in propulsion, reproduction, digestion or simply keeping afloat. The siphonophore, *Athorybia,* hangs below a rose-coloured float. Its feeding and reproductive polyps are protected behind clear flaps. Protruding between these there are gaudy orange tentacles with a battery of stinging cells that can paralyse small fish in seconds – many leptocephali will be caught in this deadly network.

The most graceful of the larger plankton spend the day in the depths but at dusk they rise to the surface where their transparent bodies take on the orange of the setting sun. These sea butterflies are sea snails modified for a free-swimming existence. Some still have external shells, while others have either no shell at all or an internal false one called a pseudo-conch. All have wing-like extensions on the sides of their bodies, which they flutter languorously; these fleshy lobes are used for feeding as well as propulsion. Bands of cilia on their surface set up currents which send small organisms streaming towards the creature's mouth.

The leptocephalus is too large to be a meal for these dainty creatures, but one kind of sea butterfly, *Gleba*, impedes her voyage. For a while the sea has the consistency of treacle and clings to the eel larva's body. She is in a sheet of mucus spun by *Gleba* to capture minute planktonic organisms. Even though *Gleba* only measures 5 centimetres across its outstretched wings, its trap can be up to 2 metres wide. When the membrane becomes clogged with food, *Gleba* draws in its catch to a mouth situated at the end of a long proboscis. The cloying liquid slows down our leptocephalus, but she has the strength to struggle free.

Gleba's net is vast compared with most objects in the plankton, but in the nekton, a category of inhabitants of the open sea defined as being powerful enough to swim in any direction, there's a fish with a mouth that's nearly as large. One of these whale sharks passes above our leptocephalus, blocking out the blue of the sky with the glaring white of its belly. This is the largest fish in the world: some whale sharks reach 18 metres in length – this one is 12. The creature cruises just below the surface with its massive mouth wide open, a close call for our eel larva because whale sharks feed on plankton. The forward momentum sweeps gallons of sea water right into its maw and straight through its fine gill rakers, which sieve out any food. The whale shark's gill slits flare open as it feeds: the resulting gaps, 40 centimetres wide, are the escape route for water flowing from the mouth. Golden trevally, small yellow fish, don't mind the gaps, darting in and out to pick off any scraps caught on the gill rakers.

Despite its size, the whale shark is harmless to everything except plankton – it does have twelve rows of teeth, but these are only 2 millimetres long. Ridges stand proud from the shark's blue and white skin, and the markings behind the gills are unique to each individual. As the leviathan disappears the sweep of its great tail produces a powerful vortex, spinning the leptocephalus southwards once more.

A year old and 6 centimetres long, our eel larva is nearing the end of this phase of her incredible journey. The East Australia current that carries her now sweeps her around the corner of a continent. In the inshore waters of the Bass Strait between the mainland and Tasmania she metamorphoses again. Her flattened leaf of a body narrows and shortens into a cylindrical needle. Her new manifestation is eel-like but still colourless and clear. Every detail of her internal structure can be seen – the delicate backbone, the pulsating heart, even blood corpuscles in the filigree of capillaries in her fins. This is why she is now called a glass eel.

She is still assisted by moving currents, but for much of the time she now swims vigorously. Hugging the coast of the state of Victoria she passes close to the Twelve Apostles, geological features of unsurpassed grandeur. These gigantic pillars of limestone soar 100 metres above the waves. Like the nearby grottoes, chimneys and arches, they were sculpted by the wild weather on this part of the coast. Any weaknesses in the limestone are exploited by the wind, rain and ocean. The blowhole is another famous feature which has been carved out by the waves. Now the sea thunders inland through a tunnel, 400 metres long.

Our glass eel senses her surroundings in several ways: sight, disturbances in the water and smell. Conditions are calm, so as well as seeing the submerged rock of the Twelve Apostles, by swimming close she can make out the limestone above the surface. Because of the way light waves behave on entering water, she has a 'window' into the atmosphere of almost 97 degrees. This window is named after the Dutch scientist, Snell, who studied the nature of light and refraction.

Somewhat like humans feeling wind against their

The whale shark trawls the ocean for plankton with a mouth that's 2 metres across. The largest fish on the planet, it can grow up to 18 metres long and weigh 40 tonnes.

cheeks, our glass eel can feel disturbances in the water caused by waves thundering towards the blowhole, or the wake left by something swimming nearby. She does this with the lateral line system under her skin, a system which is shared with other fish. Each organ on the lateral line contains a lump of jelly, and if one of these bends because of water ripples a message is sent to the brain. This sense is also used as a short-range warning system. If the pattern of water flowing around swimming fish is distorted by an obstacle, the disturbance is detected by the lateral line organs of the head. This is the way fish avoid bumping into the glass walls of aquariums.

Our eel also has an acute sense of smell and, by using information from chemicals dissolved in water, she searches for the mouth of a river. The one she finds has beaches of golden sand on both sides. In the vastness of the open sea she came

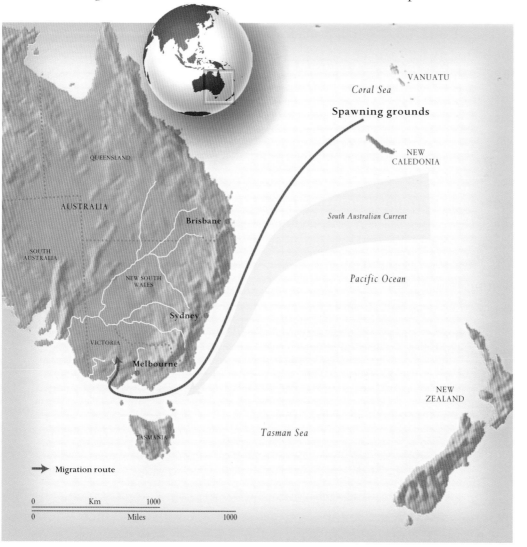

into contact with few of her kind, but millions of glass eels congregate here. Most were spawned when she was, but others travelled more slowly and hatched in the previous season. During the day the massed glass eels bide their time, waiting for the right conditions to head upstream. Millions more have already converged, or are converging in estuaries all over Tasmania and south-east Australia. They're not returning in the same way as salmon, which are born in fresh water and return to the place where they were spawned. Glass eels have never been in rivers before, and it's unlikely that they choose the same watercourse in which their parents matured; more probably they are distributed randomly by the vagaries of the currents that carry them.

Swaying gently amongst the vivid green algae, our glass eel is secure. Bobbing wavelets reshape and distort the shafts of sunlight which chase each other over the rocks and sand. Every so often shadows fall across the glass eel as shapes glide on the boundary between air and sea – surfers, paddling their boards out to breaking waves. The eel sinks deeper into cover when another moving object causes a disturbance in the water, a bather kicking off only 30 centimetres away. As the girl passes overhead, her toe brushes the algae. Most of the human beach-goers are unaware of the miniature eels that mass in the shallows every spring.

It's November and the last quarter of the moon. In this lunar phase conditions are perfect for glass eels to move. The high tide is at or soon after dusk: the rising water helps push them upstream, there is minimal moonshine and the darkness shields the glass eels from gulls and most other fishing birds.

Our glass eel leaves the cover of the algae as the sun dips below the horizon. The estuary bottom is dangerous and concealed in the mud there is a minefield. Waiting in ambush there are fish called tupong. A pair of small eyes are all that is visible: they're close together and on the top of the predator's head. Leaf litter and silt cover the rest of its 20-centimetre-long body. The tupong senses the approach of the first glass eels to its lair.

It twitches a pectoral fin and a leaf skeleton falls away, but because of its camouflage colours of reddish brown marbled with greenish brown it cannot be seen. The glass eels are now directly above the yellow eyes. Suddenly a huge mouth opens and snaps shut. Two glass eels are trapped inside; another two writhe in the tupong's rubbery lips before they too are swallowed. Our glass eel swims through a cloud of silt, the aftermath of the tupong explosion.

Tupong are generalized carnivores which feed on anything they can cram into their mouths. They are common in the estuary and will engulf many more glass eels before the migration is over. Other predatory fish also cash in on the bonanza. Estuary perch, olive green with silver backs, are chasers, not pouncers. With scales flashing as they twist and lunge, large ones, some weighing as much as 4 kilograms, weave in and out of groups of glass eels. With their not inconsiderable gapes the perch swallow the eels as though they were wriggling spaghetti. Eels lay prodigious numbers of eggs to compensate for this huge mortality rate: if just two of the progeny survive, the maintenance of the population is assured.

Glass eels travelling on either side are snapped up, but our eel escapes the attention of predators. The next morning she hides in a stand of submerged rush; within a single square metre there are a thousand others of her kind. Glass eels travel individually and are not believed to form coordinated shoals, but even so when there are countless thousands on the move they can never be alone.

Nobody knows why some of them will stay in the estuary for a year or two while others, like our glass eel, press upstream as soon as they can. She makes good progress, and within a fortnight she is away from any tidal influence. From now on she and the others must forge upstream against the water's flow without help from currents or a rising tide. She travels mainly with other females now, as most male freshwater eels drop away to stay and mature in the lower reaches of the river.

After a short time in fresh water the appearance of our glass eel changes once again. For the first time she develops coloration and becomes a sandy-grey brown on her back and sides and a paler creamy brown below. Now she is called an elver, and she begins to eat voraciously. To cope with this her stomach enlarges, and a loop develops in her intestine. En route she feeds whenever she can, snaffling up crustaceans, molluscs, worms and insects.

When she swims, muscular waves undulate along her body from head to tail. As they sweep downwards, each wave displaces water and the resulting forces propel the elver forward. She is not able to swim up an unbroken swift rush of water and must choose a route where the flow is at its lowest. If riffles or rapids stretch across the river from bank to bank, our elver uses her lateral line to sense local variations in the water velocity. In this way she negotiates most watery obstacles with ease, but ahead there is a barrier that she will have to be at her most tenacious to overcome.

It's January and our elver is now the size of a pencil. She enters a stretch of river where the current has slowed to nothing and there's a log jam of elvers. They cram into every nook, cranny, crevice and crack, yet she manages to find a cleft where there's room for one more. In favoured retreats, a line of a hundred heads sway gently in what little water movement there is. Mouths open and close at high frequency – there's little oxygen here, and a greater volume of water needs to be drawn over the gills if the elvers are to absorb enough. In some shallower areas they are packed so densely that fins, tails or heads occasionally break the surface.

Some elvers swim in open water in broad daylight. An over-riding urge to forge upstream causes this restlessness – some of them have been here for up to a month. But stopping them, rising almost vertically from the river and in stark contrast to nature's abstract arrangement of rocks and boulders, is the smooth grey wall of a dam. For the elvers this is as inhospitable as a desert – a moonscape of bone-dry concrete and sun-scorched algae. They can leave the water for the land, but they need moisture. This is a river modified by man, as are most in Australia. The demands of agriculture in this thirsty landscape mean that in the spring, when the rivers should be naturally in spate, so much water is diverted for irrigation that they are reduced to a mere trickle or dry up completely. When the farmers' demand is less, engineers allow the rivers to flow again, but this may be a season removed from the natural state of affairs. This manipulation of water has a great impact on all river life. For instance, some native Australian fish need the stimulus of rising water temperatures to breed in spring. If water is moved up and down the river artificially it doesn't have a chance to stand and warm up in the sun. Without this trigger, the fishes' calendar goes out of kilter and they spawn

Carnivorous estuary perch can weigh up to 10 kilograms. Their diet includes shrimps, worms and molluscs. They will also take the opportunity to fill their stomachs with elvers when the young eels migrate upstream.

at the wrong time, if at all. It also puts a stop to the seasonal inundation of wet-lands, limiting the regions where waterbirds can breed. And, of course, the lack of water causes elver migrations to falter; some dams, for example the Derwent Weir power station complex on the Tamar river at Launceston in Tasmania, is so massive that it stops any upstream migration completely. The Fisheries Department have to net the elvers and take them further upriver in a lorry .

Predators make the most of these enforced stops, and accessible elvers are picked off by the most unlikely fishermen. A pair of magpie larks, one of the most familiar and ubiquitous of Australian birds, scrutinize the shallows. Both sexes have bold piebald plumage; the male has a white eyebrow which is lacking in the female, who instead has a pure white forehead and throat. The bulk of their diet consists of insects, but now they paddle at the edge of the water before striking down and pulling out an elver. They walk sedately between favourite fishing spots, bobbing their heads back and forth in time with their feet.

A more famous Australian bird behaves unusually at the weir, plunging repeatedly to seize elvers from the shallows. Each time the bird flutters down there is a chocolate brown and white blur and then a splash before it flaps laboriously back to its perch. Before swallowing the elvers it stuns them. Kookaburras are the largest of the eighty-five species of kingfisher in the world, but for them the family name is a misnomer since they rarely fish. More usually they perch and then pounce onto solid ground to grab insects, snakes, lizards and rodents.

Once again, sheer weight of numbers gives protection to our elver. Like the predatory perch and tupong, the birds have so much choice that the risk of an individual elver being caught is low, but these odds will increase when the elvers begin their assault on the face of the dam. In the last few days there has been torrential rain farther up the river's course. Water has been released from other man-made impoundments and in the late afternoon it flows towards the massed elvers.

At dusk, almost imperceptibly at first, water begins to trickle through cracks and over the lowest points of the dam. The desperate elvers sense the moisture and some begin to climb up the dampness. When the flow increases, their attempt to scale the 3-metre-high wall fails and they're swept back. By nightfall the dam has disappeared behind a curtain of fast-flowing water, white and silver in the moonlight. The elvers can't cope with the brutal velocity on the main face, but somehow they must find a way to overcome this obstacle.

If it's a hot day tomorrow, the demands from irrigation could dry up the river until autumn. Our elver joins a procession swimming towards the only option. Where the dam abuts the river bank there is a splash zone of damp concrete.

Already a shiny rope of eels climbs upwards. Rapidly flicking her tail, our elver leaps right out of the tumbling water and foam. Her slimy body makes contact with the wall and she sticks.

Then a broad-winged, short-tailed creature with the appearance of a great bat glides in to land at the water's edge. Our elver braces the curves of her body against irregularities in the concrete and levers herself forward. A cloud swallows the moon and a hunched shape looms over her. A metre-high, dagger-billed bird stops and stands motionless on creamy yellow legs. The rufous night heron has a bluish black crown, a back with cinnamon tones and a belly of delicate white. Our elver wriggles upwards in the slimy procession. The moon is uncovered and the heron is still as a statue; only its pupils, which now contract to reveal the bright yellow rings of its iris, show that it's alive. Higher up the wall an elver loses its grip and falls. The mighty jabbing bill accelerates straight down. Our elver is knocked out of the way by the faller, just before the bird's mandibles close around her body. Both young eels plummet into the river and swim away through the heron's splayed toes.

The moving shadow of the bird causes other elvers to drop. When it recoils and jabs again the bird makes no mistake. Soon it has filled its crop with food and it heads for the heronry in a stand of paper bark trees. Back at the nest it coughs up a mass of freshly killed elvers for its chicks.

Our elver's urge to migrate compels her to attempt to surmount the dam once more. Climbing with the elvers there are whitebait, the local name for juvenile galaxiids. There are more species of these minnow-like fish – about twenty – than of any other fish group in Australian fresh waters. The galaxiids now climbing the weir are of a species that spend about six months at sea, not far offshore, before returning to spawn in the river's upper reaches – this is exactly the reverse of what eels do. On hatching, their young will be washed out to sea just as their parents were.

Unlike the elvers, the galaxiids ascend the dam in rapid bursts, spreading their fins and wiggling vigorously. After an hour of tenacious climbing our elver is passed by many galaxiids, but eventually she reaches the main river above the dam and forges upstream. Tens of thousands will make the ascent tonight: from dusk until long after dawn, the damp surface of the concrete gleams with elvers.

The next morning our elver's retreat is a tangle of spindly roots which pro-trude from the creek bank. Amongst the roots there are two holes in the bank, just above the water level; by one of them is a flat stone strewn with crayfish remains, mussel shells and fish bones. This is the feeding table of the occupant of one of the burrows, a large rodent about 60 centimetres long including the tail.

The neighbouring burrow houses different creatures. The adult is about half the size of a household cat, and they belong to the strange group of mammals which lay eggs and are called monotremes. There are only three species: two are echidnas or spiny anteaters, which live on land, and the third is the platypus. Both of the tunnels in the bank were originally excavated by a female platypus, arguably the most uniquely Australian mammal.

The burrow which she frequents was constructed specifically for nesting and is an elaborate affair with many branches. At the end of one of these there is a chamber containing a nest of leaves and grasses. In early October she laid two eggs which hatched after ten days. Nourished on milk secreted from glands in her abdomen, her babies are now quite large and in another month they'll be able to fend for themselves. For much of the day they curl up with their mother and sleep. She'll begin to forage at dusk.

Over a thirty-month period the female platypus has excavated eighteen different tunnels, most of them simple resting burrows about 2 metres long. One of these has been commandeered by a water rat and her four babies. Water rats are also native Australians. They are 60 centimetres long with brown fur and a white-tipped tail (they are totally unrelated to the European water rat, which is in fact a vole). Platypus breed only once in a season, but this is the rat's fourth litter. The two platypus babies are well advanced, and this evening they'll follow their mother into the water for the first time.

The sun has dropped below the level of the paper barks and the river is in deep shade. Elvers are already swimming past the tangle of roots when a pliable, rubbery bill attached to a body of dense brown fur and a flattened, paddle-like tail slips silently into the river. The platypus executes a rolling dive and submerges. Underwater her eyes are closed, and information about her surroundings comes from sensory cells in the skin of her bill. Her webbed front feet propel her forward and our elver detects the currents they produce as the platypus swims past.

The platypus passes straight through a concentration of elvers. She's fast but not that fast, and rarely catches fish in open water. On the bottom she uses her sensitive bill to poke about under pebbles and rocks. If an elver was concealed there she could snaffle it up, but the bulk of her food consists of slower-moving adult and larval invertebrates, particularly shrimps and crayfish. Special receptors in her bill detect the body electricity of her prey. Soon her large cheek pouches are full and she rises up to the surface. As she chews her food, the platypus floats with all four legs extended. After leaving the root tangle, our elver can make out the shape of the platypus above her silhouetted against the moon.

The platypus detects prey, mainly small worms and crustaceans, with receptors in its bill. Food is collected in large cheek pouches before being chewed and swallowed at the surface.

Elvers must surmount obstacles such as Werribee dam in Victoria on their runs upstream. They're beaten back by fast flowing water and have to wait for nightfall to begin their assault.

The elvers climb in their thousands in the splash zone at the edge of the dam. Clambering up the 9 metres of concrete, they lever the curves in their bodies against any irregularity in the dam's surface.

Suddenly a silvery missile heads straight towards our elver. She darts forward as the water rat lunges, and has enough acceleration to shoot into a hollow log. A pink-clawed hand scrabbles at the entrance but our elver works her way into a cleft that's too narrow for her pursuer. In less than a second the water rat is gone – there are plenty more elvers that are easier to catch. Her white-tipped tail flows behind her as she heads towards a thousand swimming near the bank. When she is immersed her pelt traps a layer of air whose bubbles give her a coat of silver. Pushing her webbed hind feet against the resistance of the water she twists and turns, looking for her quarry, and before long she has an elver in her mouth.

Her babies play and mock fight in the shallows as they aren't confident in the deep water yet. When their mother drops the stunned elver near them, a slimy tug of war ensues. One of them eventually wrestles the prize away and clambers onto the feeding table to eat its meal. This is the first of more than sixty elvers that the adult water rat will catch for her litter this night.

Our elver slips away while the rat makes the most of a bonanza spawned in the Pacific over 3000 kilometres away. After weeks of sustained swimming our elver is near the farthest reaches of the river system. The high rainfall means that most of the watery connections between the river and ponds, lakes and billabongs – river branches that come to a dead end – are flowing. She makes the most of this opportunity and deviates from the main river, heading down a muddy stream. This leads her into a huge productive lake, full of luxuriant vegetation and rich with crustaceans and aquatic insects.

For now our elver's wanderings are over: she'll settle here where there's an abundance of food and cover to conceal her from predators. Now she must grow and grow to become an eel. At present she's still no larger than a pencil, but before she returns to the ocean she could be well over a metre long and weigh nearly 7 kilograms. To get to this stage and become a mature sea-going eel, she'll need to survive in the lake for over fifteen years.

During her lengthy time here, she comes into contact with many of the lake's creatures. Some can be eaten, while for others she could become the meal. As she gets larger the numbers in the latter category dwindle, until by the time she's fully grown only three types of animal can trouble her.

Over the years our eel watches the lake and its inhabitants. On most days she lurks in a favourite snag of twigs and branches. Through the water surface, unless it is ruffled by wind and rain, she sees the shapes of the red gum trees, extending some 10 metres above the bank. They aren't deciduous, and the overall impression of the leaves is always the same. The bark, in contrast, presents a shifting kaleidoscope of colours depending upon the weather and time of day. Before a storm the straight trunk and intricate whorl of branches take on the brooding darkness of the clouds; at dawn and at dusk, if the day is fine, they are pinkish or orange brown; and when the sun is high they're burnt out, a brilliant white against the solid blue of the sky. In front of the snag a patch of open water merges imperceptibly with the crowded vertical stems of water lilies whose leaves, which in spring and summer are interspersed with huge white blooms, float in rafts on the surface.

Among the myriad waterbirds, only the largest herons and cormorants are a threat once our eel has grown over 30 centimetres in length. Waterfowl are common, and amongst their number there are some unique Australians. The pink-eared duck, probably the most unusual duck in the world, gets its name from a small fleshy pink patch behind its eyes. Black and white striped plumage give it an alternative name, the zebra duck. Dense chirruping flocks land above our eel and cruise along with their beaks immersed and water up to their eyes. Flaps of skin at the sides turn their bills into broad scoops: water is taken in and any planktonic food filtered out by an arrangement of fine plates, then the cleaned water is pumped out of the sides of the bill and back into the lake.

Another extraordinary duck, the musk duck, sometimes dives past our eel's retreat when searching for aquatic insects, snails or frogs, staying submerged for over a minute. Both sexes of this duck have dusky black upperparts overlaid with numerous striations of creamy white, while their bellies are white mottled with grey. Hanging under his bill the male has a huge pendulous bladder which he uses during a remarkable courtship display. This begins in March and reaches a peak in September; throughout this time our eel can probably detect the bird's presence through chemicals in the water. These secretions give the musk duck his characteristic scent and originate from the preen gland on his rump. The odour becomes intense during the breeding season.

The territory of the musk duck nearest to our eel includes the open water between the bank and the water lily patch, and this is where he performs his display. With exaggerated kicks he sails into the middle and then stops. Next he uses his webbed feet to send out jets of water 2 metres or more behind him. Now he raises his head and blows out his neck and cheeks. This inflates the bladder under his bill to a diameter of 15 centimetres or more. Then, while emitting a piercing whistle, he raises his tail feathers and spreads them in a fan over his back before

*Short-finned eels may spend up to fifteen
years in fresh water before returning
3000 kilometres to the Pacific where they were
spawned. Adult females can grow over a metre
long and weigh as much as 7 kilograms.*

*This Australian lake in the state of Victoria is
an ideal place for short-finned eels to grow and
mature. The eels lurk in the snags of twigs and
branches formed by the red gum trees that
fringe the water.*

sinking low into the water to revolve slowly. If his water sports attract a female, he climbs on to her back to mate. As he plays no role in nest-building, incubation or rearing of the young, he can have several partners in a season.

When the musk duck's display season is tailing off, the blue billed duck's is beginning. In this species, the drake and duck look different. To set off a beak of vivid blue, the male has a glossy black head and neck with a rich chestnut body; the female is brown with a grey-brown bill. These ducks are furtive by nature and the water lily leaves often screen their courtship, but the vibrations from the spectacular display pass through the water and are detected by our eel's lateral line. First the drake splashes a spume of water backwards; then he springs erect, virtually standing on his tail, while vibrating his bill up and down. Sprints across the water with flailing feet and wings, and rocking to and fro with his tail feathers held erect in a fan, are also part of his repertoire. After a vigorous chase above and below water, he overtakes and copulates with his mate. On one occasion the copulating pair are completely submerged only a metre from our eel's lair.

It's in the late evening when the ducks start to roost that our eel becomes active. She'll feed all through the night, but generally her stomach is at its fullest between 3 and 6 a.m. She glides from the snag and swims slowly along the lake bottom, stopping periodically to thrust her snout into soft sediment to search for worms or insect larvae. She often investigates a limestone outcrop because there are hidden crayfish there which are undetectable to many other hunters. Again our eel's lateral line receptors come into their own. Like a kind of long-range touch, they sense the slightest movement of crustacean leg or claw. Once the prey has given itself away, it is always a tight squeeze to reach it, but the slimy, stream-lined, stripped down body of our eel maximizes her ability to negotiate narrow spots.

Freshwater eels don't have the sticking out, paired pectoral and pelvic fins of other fish, or their bulging gill covers, which are reduced to a small hole in eels. The copious slime produced by eels also helps them to thread their way through the narrowest of gaps. When our eel reaches a crayfish, it is either dragged out to be swallowed or, if there is room, gulped down in situ. Her diet changes with age and size: when she is less than half a metre long it consists primarily of small invertebrates, snails, crayfish, shrimps and the like. Above half a metre she feeds extensively on fish. To catch these she glides slowly just above the bottom and surprises them while they sleep.

Hiding by day and feasting by night is the routine for much of the year, although for a month or two in winter temperatures become too cool for such activity. Our eel then swims backward and digs, tail first, into the soft bottom sediments. She passes into a torpid state and lives off her fat reserves, staying buried until the water temperature exceeds 10 degrees centigrade.

At any time of year our eel rarely reveals herself during the day – in all her years in the lake she only does this four times. These occasions are after floods, when she makes the most of land-based animal foods that have been washed into the water. On these forays to gorge on earthworms she encounters an extraordinary reptile. Snake-necked turtles are amazing because they can cram a 20-centimetre neck inside their chocolate brown carapace, which is only 10 centimetres long. They use their necks to reach out for food, and as a periscope to lift a pair of nostrils to the surface to breathe. When resting or disturbed, the turtles fold their necks into a horizontal 'S' to take them back into the shell.

When our eel feeds alongside the turtles they cut up worms with their horny jaws, while she sucks the worms in like spaghetti. Our eel lacks the ability to cut or nibble, because her jaw muscles are weak and her teeth, although numerous, are small and round with no cutting edges. But she doesn't always have the option to swallow a meal in one go. She's a consummate scavenger and to dismember large food items she 'spins' for her supper.

One night when she is about eighteen years old, she follows a scent trail to the body of a possum which after dying of old age has fallen into the water. As well as our short-finned eel, the corpse has attracted other short-fins from all over the lake. They seethe all over the carrion. Our eel noses her way through the mass until she can grasp some flesh. It's loosely attached, so by pulling back she tears off a mouthful. In this situation, because of the continuous fin along their back, around their tails and along their belly, eels have an advantage over other fish. With this arrangement they can swim palindromically – they move backwards just as well as forwards. Most fish can only pull backwards weakly by sculling with their pectoral fins, but eels can swim backwards forcefully, using all their body weight to maximize their pulling power.

Our eel grasps another piece of meat that is firmly attached. It won't detach by jerking or pulling, so the eel resorts to spinning. Before going into a spin she grips tightly. As she twists, each point of her straightened body rotates simultaneously. She revolves with dizzying speed and her white belly flashes in the gloom. Her momentum is such that she achieves a rate of fourteen spins per second – Olympic-class ice skaters rarely achieve more than five or six. The exact mechanism of how eels spin is a mystery: internal pumping of body fluids probably generates the force, while uniquely elastic fibres store and release this energy to complete each rotation. Our eel achieves twenty-five revolutions in a three-second bout of spinning, to pull off a chunk of meat the right size to swallow. Over a dozen eels jerk, pull, twist and spin, and the commotion attracts a monster. Our eel is in great danger. She has been detected by the only denizen of the lake that can swallow her whole.

In precisely the same way that she approaches her own prey, a monstrous fish stalks our eel. The creature is immense, the length and girth of a tall man. It was spawned in the Pacific and, although it arrived a decade earlier, its route to this lake was the same as that of our eel. Most of its kind are in river systems to the east: this is one of only a handful in western Victoria, and the only one in the lake. Its fins extend further round its body than those of the short-finned species, which is why it's called the long-finned eel.

To avoid sending out vibrations that would give it away, the long-fin slowly glides closer. Our eel has found a chunk of carrion and is oblivious to the threat. The long-fin stops to flex its head downwards. Still preoccupied with food, our eel begins to spin. Distracted by a swirl of stimuli around her head and lateral line, she's even less alert to the approaching danger. The long-fin's thick, rubbery lips and huge mouth are less than 15 centimetres away. Our eel stops its spin and, just as the long-fin lunges, jerks the carrion to one side. The giant grabs the possum flesh instead of its intended prey and, letting go of her hard-earned meal, our eel hurtles backwards, escaping behind a curtain of filamentous weed.

Our eel remains in the lake for the next seven years, but never comes into contact with the long-fin again. After a quarter of a century in fresh water she begins her final transformation. Her skin, eyes and internal organs all begin to change, but these changes are not very far advanced before heavy autumn rains trigger her urge to travel once again. She swims back to the river along the same stream which brought her to the lake all those years ago.

The rise in river level has stimulated many mature short-fins to migrate. Everywhere landlocked pools and lakes overflow, allowing eels access to a downstream route. On a favourable night, when the sky is at its darkest at the time of the new moon, our eel travels fin to fin in a dense concentration. The journey is far less laborious than when she was an elver; she is larger now and a more powerful swimmer. With a current on her tail, in just twenty-four hours she covers 50 kilometres. The dam is no obstacle now. The river rushes over the concrete face, so she simply drops off the top, tail first. Below, the churning water bashes her against the rocks that gave her sanctuary as an elver, but she is resilient and swims on unharmed.

As she nears the estuary the physical changes that began in the lake are nearly complete. These changes prepare her for the last phase of her life, an incredible journey back to the distant spawning grounds. In the lake her coloration was olive green above and greyish white below; now her upperparts are greenish bronze and her belly is a distinct metallic silver-grey. This new silvery appearance will provide better camouflage in the open ocean. Her head has changed too: it's become sharper, almost chisel-shaped, probably to make her more streamlined for sustained swimming. Remarkably, her eyes have enlarged one and a half times and there are changed pigments inside. Adult eels probably migrate at great depths in the ocean; in these dimly lit waters, bigger eyes would enhance their vision. The actual quality of the light changes in the deep too – the water absorbs all wavelengths except blue, and a different array of visual pigments means under these conditions the eel can see well.

Further changes are now occurring inside our eel's body. Nothing, even prey, must distract from her prodigious migration, so her gut shrinks and she ceases to feed. To minimize water loss in the salt water

As the skin of the eel hasn't come off cleanly, one of the competitors in the world eel-skinning championships in Branxholme, Victoria, resorts to skinning his entry with his teeth.

even her anus constricts. White, frilled, ribbon-like organs are beginning to grow along her abdomen: these are her ovaries, and their percentage of her total body weight will increase enormously as her journey progresses. She will risk everything to reach the spawning grounds ripe with eggs, so most of her body reserves will be used to fuel this fantastic voyage and to develop up to eight million eggs.

We can only speculate about why short-finned eels and most other freshwater eels travel so far to spawn. It could simply be that their nursery needs to be at a specific temperature, pressure and salinity, conditions that are only found far from landmasses. Another possibility is that their migrations are an artefact of history: 130 million years ago, when these fish arose, the distribution of the continents and oceans was quite different from today. When the landmasses began to spread apart, the narrow body of water between them grew larger and larger and even though they had to swim farther and farther to get there, the eels could have stayed faithful to their original breeding site.

Tagging migrating eels has enabled zoologists to calculate how long their marathon swim will take. Now at the river mouth our eel has another six months of travel ahead of her – if she goes at all. The river is blocked by a narrow bar of sand and gravel. Other eels have been held up and the massive accumulation forms into a solid, squirming mass. Tonight the sea is calm, so waves aren't breaking across the bar. Once they do, and the bar is wet, the eels will be able to slither across and into the sea.

Many of them, however, won't get this chance and their migration will end prematurely. Thwarted by the sandbar, our eel swims on the bottom of the estuary hither and thither. Here she comes to another barrier, this time a wall of netting. Rather than swimming over or around this wall, she moves along it for a few metres before passing through a circular metal hoop. Four of these hoops form the support for the trap. Still exploring, she continues into a funnel which opens out into a rectangular inner opening. She passes through and is now enclosed in what eel fishermen call the 'parlour'. Ahead, attached to the outer wall of the net, between the third and fourth hoops, is a vertical slit. To pass through our eel must push it open, but she is wary now and turns away. The vibrations of struggling eels already caught pulsate through the water. She turns around in the parlour but keeps swimming into dead ends. The rectangular inner opening of the outer funnel that led her here is held away from the sides of the trap, supported by strings attached to a hoop, making it difficult to escape from the parlour. After failing to find an exit our eel eventually returns to the slit and pushes her way into the toe end of the fyke-net. Over 100 other eels have already been caught; many have snouts that are raw and bloody from constantly pushing against the mesh – there is no escape.

The next morning two fishermen arrive in an aluminium dinghy. First they pull out the metal poles that anchor the fyke-net to the bottom, then they bring the trap on board. Because there is such a huge weight of eels to haul in at the toe end, both men are needed. They pull a purse string, once the end is in the dinghy, which lets the eels slide out. They form a slithering, wriggling, flapping carpet, that glistens in the sun. With a deft touch that only comes with years of handling eels, the men sort their slimy cargo. Our eel feels the heat of human fingers just behind her head. To stop her extricating herself from his grasp as he lifts her into a mesh sack, the fishermen gently kinks her body. Eels below 30 centimetres are classed as undersized and are thrown back into the estuary. Another dozen fyke-nets are emptied and reset before the bulging bags of eels are transferred into a pick-up truck and taken to the factory. In Victoria the annual catch of eels averages more than 200 tonnes and is the basis for a \$3 million industry. Ninety-five per cent of the catch is exported to Europe and South-East Asia. Our eel spends the final three days of her life in a holding tank of fresh water – it takes that long to purge the muddy flavour from her flesh. Most of the eels are taken to a cold store: if their body temperature is lowered they become torpid and die. Then they are exported to be smoked, fried or jellied. The fate of our eel is rather more unusual. She is taken from the holding tank and placed in a polythene bag filled with salt. The salt absorbs the moisture from her skin and she soon suffocates and dies. Her body is taken by truck to become part of a bizarre Australian tradition.

Each year in March, the town of Branxholme in Victoria plays host to the event. In 1980, Lynn 'Lightning' Millard was undisputed champion for the third consecutive time. When asked how he found the competition he said, 'Everybody here's as keen as mustard. I reckon eel-skinning is about to take off as a world sport.' The bushwhackers' carnival has sheepdog trials, tugs of war, whip-cracking, highland dancing, egg-catching contests and much more, but the main event is the world eel-skinning championship. The rules are simple: as quickly as possible, the eels must be gutted and prepared. Skinning aids must be approved by the judge. Most contestants use a sharp knife and their teeth. 'Lightning' Millard has skinned a pair in 50.6 seconds.

The body of our eel is in the Grand Final. In a blur of knife and hands her head and gut are removed. Her skin won't come off cleanly so the competitor lifts her body to his lips and peels off any stubborn fragments of her skin with his teeth. It's unlikely that he or the spectators have any idea of what an incredible traveller she was.

Spring sunshine in their mountain retreat in Mexico stimulates millions of monarch butterflies to fill the skies.

4

THE BUTTERFLY'S MIGRATION

H IGH ON A MOUN-
tain in Mexico is
a magical forest
of majestic oyamel
pines. It is a cool
morning in mid-March. Some of the trees seem
unusual – their shape and colour aren't what you
would expect of a pine. This is because their
branches and trunks have a dense covering of
monarch butterflies (*Danaus plexippus*). At this temperature all the insects are immobile, with closed
wings. The tiers of slumbering insects are a sombre
beige, the colour of the underside of their wings.
There are forty million butterflies in this one
colony, which is awe-inspiring enough, but as they
warm up the real magic will begin.

Sunlight filters through the trees and, as the

103

rays play on the butterflies, they open their wings, flashing the vivid orange inside. This colour is the reason they were given their name by seventeenth-century settlers in North America. So impressed were they by this magnificent butterfly that they named it 'Monarch', in honour of William of Orange, Stadtholder of Holland and later King William III of England. The patches of fiery orange begin to pulsate as the butterflies warm their flight muscles by vibrating their wings. Then, ready for coordinated flight, they explode from the trees, filling the air like a ticker-tape parade. The whisper of hundreds of thousands of wings sounds like the soft patter of spring rain. Some of the monarchs mate in swarms while others flutter to a stream to drink, but by 4 p.m. most have returned to the trees.

A female monarch roosts high up in the canopy. To be here she has completed an amazing flight of over 4000 kilometres from Canada. Tomorrow she and millions of others will begin an exodus from these mountains, and rivulets of butterflies will stream northward to re-populate the eastern United States and Canada. This monarch invasion happens each summer. Next autumn, if all goes according to plan, the descendants of our female monarch, in a migration unmatched by any other in the insect world, will return to this precise destination in Mexico.

At noon the next day, leaving the forested slopes behind, our monarch drops down into a wide valley. There's a scatter of farms, each with a red-tiled farmhouse, chickens, cows and a mule. She has two priorities – to mate and feed. Flying lower, she heads for the weedy margin of a field of maize. So confident is she in the precision of her flight as she approaches an inflorescence packed with yellow flowers, on landing her proboscis is already uncoiled. All butterflies have this hollow flexible feeding tube for imbibing liquid, which is the only kind of food that they take as adults. Our monarch drains one flower of its nectar, then, to save time coiling and uncoiling, uses the muscles in her head to lift the whole proboscis like a crane, raising it and then lowering it into an adjacent flower.

Her sense of smell is acute and quite different from that of humans. Nerve cells which open at the surface through tiny pores are the organs of smell; these can be packed together all over the surface of olfactory pegs and hairs, or in hollow pits. The antennae of our monarch, her main site of smell, are particularly richly endowed with 3700 leaf-like pegs, 2500 longer pegs and 65 hollow pit organs, all covered in chemical detectors. The reason that she can have so many is that her feelers are completely unscaled – the antennae of most other species of butterfly have a covering of scales except on the club or nudum at the end.

As well as responding to the honey smell, which is essential for feeding, our monarch is attracted to the chemicals produced by certain types of orchid. These mimic the aphrodisiac perfume that the males of closely related butterflies produce during courtship. This is apparently a remnant behaviour from the past, when male monarchs used these perfumes to woo mates; today they court with much less finesse. In fact courtship in monarchs has virtually disappeared, as in the mass aggregations at the overwintering sites there is little chance of mating with the wrong species so elaborate preliminaries are unnecessary. There is a possibility of mix-ups in the summer, but the risk is negligible. Male monarchs stay near to the plants where the females lay their eggs, and in most areas female monarchs far outnumber the females of any similar butterfly nearby.

A patrolling male darts towards our female as she feeds. He looks much the same as her except he has a conspicuous black mark on each hindwing. In other butterflies these areas produce quantities of aphrodisiac, but male monarchs produce only small amounts. A nudge encourages her into the air. He follows and grabs her. The pair spiral to the ground. He touches her with his antennae to make sure his gender identification is correct, and after he is certain, they mate. He holds her abdomen with powerful claspers at the end of his and takes off with the female dangling behind. This 'post-nuptial' flight takes the pair to the top of a shrubby bush where they stay in tandem for over an hour.

The female has already mated with another male at the overwintering site, but it's to her advantage to mate again. As well as ensuring that she receives enough viable sperm, it also gives her an energy boost. The male's sperm are wrapped in a parcel of protein and fat which she absorbs for the demands of migration and egg production. Once the male has released her, our monarch continues her unhurried flight, supping from flowers along the route.

If she gets the chance, she rides the persistent strong winds which blow from the south. She doesn't need to rush, because her eggs are not yet fully formed. They only began to develop when there are more than eleven hours of daylight and temperatures are approaching 20 degrees centigrade. Every afternoon she seeks a place in which to spend the night, usually at the top of a small tree.

In early April, our monarch glides over some reeds fringing an expanse of sun-speckled water. The bank of the Rio Grande that she leaves is in Mexico, while the one at which she arrives is in the United States. On a rising current of air she soars over a square building, blinding white in the sun. Today, there are tourists, but when her ancestors passed this way over 160 years ago the Alamo was besieged. In this part of Texas there were heavy rains earlier in the year, and now the roadside verges are a multicoloured tapestry of spring flowers. Our monarch's flight is leisurely, with regular stops to examine blooms for their

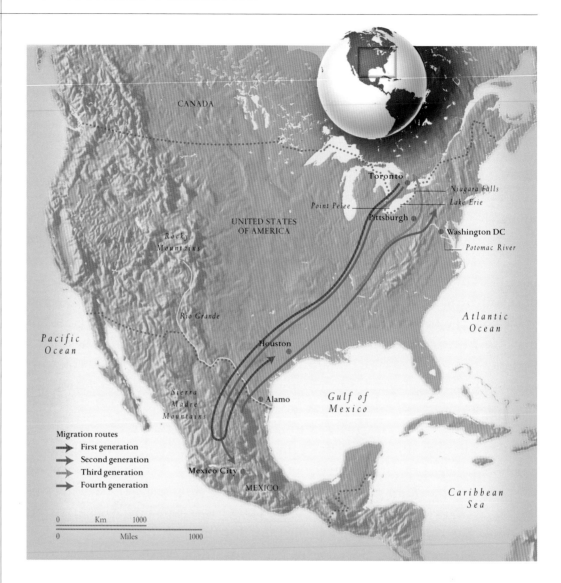

Migration routes
→ First generation
→ Second generation
→ Third generation
→ Fourth generation

nectar potential and leaves for their food-plant potential. Now she is ready to offload some of her 400 eggs.

The monarch is searching for milkweeds in the genus *Asclepias*, which includes about 108 species distributed over much of North America. She could lay her eggs on any of these, but some are difficult to find and others are rare. The first species she comes across is commonly named antelope horn. It has large pinkish-white flowers about 3 centimetres across and broad, flat leaves which are arranged on the stem in a whorl. Our monarch alights on one of the plants and drums her forelegs on a leaf. These have chemical receptors like her antennae, so she can taste

Monarchs are the largest butterflies in North America, with a wing span of 8-10 centimetres. The males (there are four in this picture) have a black mark on each of their hindwings.

with her legs if the plant is the right kind. As it is, she curls her abdomen and lays her first egg on the underside of a tender young leaf. The yellow capsule is about a millimetre long with a shell exquisitely sculpted with bumps and ridges, so its surface is broken up into a honeycomb of cells. Our butterfly repeats the process on other milkweed plants in the patch. For good reason she only lays one egg per plant. The fortunes of the four eggs which she deposits here will be mixed.

The day is beginning to heat up. Down the ruler-straight road, far in the distance, a red and silver apparition wobbles in the shimmering heat. After depositing egg number four, she leaves the patch of milkweeds and takes off to scout for more. The apparition is closer now; it kills a yellow butterfly, a bee and a beetle in quick succession. Our monarch's flightpath takes her over the tarmacadam. An ant-lion and praying mantis smash into the road cruiser's grille of shiny chrome.

Evolution hasn't prepared any insects for 20-tonne objects travelling into a headwind at 100 kilometres per hour. Sun flashes off the grille which is spattered with the bodies of victims. The road cruiser is so close that sensory hairs on our monarch's back detect the vibrations of its engine. Then a thermal of warm air rises from the road and takes her up and over the cab. Our monarch is buffeted in the dust cloud in the road cruiser's wake. The largest fragments tear her wings, but her flight isn't impaired. Cars and lorries are one of the major man-made killers of monarchs in North America today.

By early May our female's wings are even more tattered from general wear and tear. She's south-west of Houston, on the prairies. On her journey through Texas she has meticulously chosen sites to lay her eggs. When the day warms up she'll flutter feebly to deposit the last few. She's spent the night perched below a thistle leaf and now she's alert to a commotion nearby.

She can hear, but not that well. Remarkably, it's thought that she, like other butterflies, perceives sound with the veins in her forewing. If this is the case, a 'vein-splitting noise' is being made only 3 metres away by some of the world's most endangered birds. The Atwater prairie chickens are making booming sounds like a foghorn. Our monarch doesn't just hear the birds, she sees them as well. Her compound eyes (so-called because each is composed of thousands of independent lensed eyes called ommatidia) are very sensitive to movement and colour — she has wrap-around vision and can see simultaneously up, forwards, down, to the sides and some way behind her.

One bird moves towards her, stomping his feet before raising feathered tufts above his head and inflating bright orange sacs on either side of his neck. These are the resonance chambers that increase the volume of his booming calls. To the left another bird flutters, leaping high into the air. The resolution of the butterfly's eyes is inferior to that of human eyes – she can see moving shapes but not the detailed patterns of brown stripes and streaks of the plumage on these hen-like birds. The prairie chickens move away. Our monarch was in no danger – her thistle merely happens to be on the edge of a display ground. The birds are males preoccupied with attracting female Atwater prairie chickens. Because of the destruction of America's native grasslands their population has been decimated to 2-3000.

As the air warms, our monarch flaps over the prairie chickens who, this late in the day, dance half-heartedly. She locates a suitable milkweed and alights. A gentle breeze begins and then dies; leaves sway gently and then are still but, on a grass stem next to our monarch, something green keeps on swaying. The creature, 10 centimetres long, isn't yet mature. After its next moult, the final one into adulthood, it will be able to mate and the wing buds which now extend down most of its back will transform into fully functional wings so it can fly. The insect holds out its forelegs in front of its body in what could be an attitude of worship. This is how praying mantises were named, but in fact they are traps waiting to be sprung.

The mantis is poised. As our monarch lowers her abdomen, its green eyes swivel towards her. As if calculating the distance to the unwary butterfly, the mantis rocks back and forth. As an egg is laid, the mantis's raptorial forelegs flash forward impaling the monarch on formidable spikes. After a while she stops struggling and the mantis eats her alive. Our monarch's papery wings, chewed through at their bases, float to the ground. After its meal the mantis cleans itself fastidiously; it wipes away an egg that stuck to its mouthparts as it ate the monarch's abdomen. The egg drops to the ground close to one of the orange wings. It will almost certainly dry out and perish before it can hatch. Even if it does hatch, the nearest milkweed leaf is too far for a young caterpillar to reach and it will starve, but what of the first four eggs laid on the roadside verge?

The weather is warm, and three of the eggs hatch after three days. The fourth is devoured by another monarch's caterpillar that hatched earlier in the season. These cannibalistic tendencies are one of the reasons why monarchs usually only lay one egg per plant. Of course they can't know if another female has got there before them unless they land on the exact leaf where she deposited her egg. Of the trio that hatch successfully, one is killed by the second meal of its life. Its first food was the remains of the eggshell from which it hatched. Then the tiny caterpillar bites into a milkweed leaf and a white fluid bubbles from the wound and swamps the larva with sticky latex. This glutinous liquid gums up its mouthparts and legs so it starves. Many larvae are killed in this fashion. The fortunate ones nibble at the portions of the leaves that happen to be less latex-rich, or are on milkweeds which have a paltry supply throughout.

Ironically, the caterpillars that survive their first few feeds gain protection from the plant's defence system. The response when their leaves are attacked gives milkweeds their common name. Their scientific name, *Asclepias*, was given them after the Greek god of healing, an indication of the high regard in which the plant has long been held in folk medicine. The medically valuable chemicals contained in milkweed are alkaloids called cardiac glycosides, which are similar to the heart drug digitoxin. Few animals feed upon milkweed because of the toxicity of these chemicals; monarch caterpillars not only feed upon them but also store the chemicals for defence.

A praying mantis has ambushed a monarch butterfly, now it devours its head and body. Mantis nymphs can't fly but their wing buds get larger after each moult; when adult, they have fully developed wings.

These cardiac glycosides aren't much help for the third of our monarch's caterpillars, which is sucked dry of body fluids before it even has time to assimilate them. It's found by a bright black and red stink bug

which plunges its stiletto-like mouthparts deep into the larva's body. The caterpillar is eaten from the inside out. Like butterflies, hemipteran bugs can only cope with fluid food – so only the liquid centre of prey can be consumed. The shrivelled skin of the caterpillar is left behind as evidence of the deed.

The fourth caterpillar of our monarch grows and grows. When it emerged from the egg it was minute – less than 2 millimetres in length – but after two weeks it was 10 centimetres long and some 3000 times its birth weight. If a 3-kilogram human baby grew at the same rate, it would weigh 9 tonnes at the end of a fortnight!

The caterpillar achieves this feat by chomping milkweed leaves with metronomic regularity, by day and night, if the weather is warm. Occasionally it pauses to rest or to moult – a body that expands as rapidly as this soon outgrows its skin. The caterpillar continues chewing while the new skin forms beneath, but stops to 'strip off' the old one. First it fastens itself to a leaf with a length of silk produced from glands just below its mouth. Once the caterpillar is secure, it swallows air and increases in size. Starting at the head, the old skin begins to split, and then the caterpillar wriggles out. It wastes little time before feeding again and it's

The monarch caterpillar has a colourful rugby-shirt-like skin to warn predators that it is poisonous. The long black filaments at the front end of its body are also for defence and are lashed in the air to startle attackers.

the discarded skin that is consumed first. All monarch caterpillars moult four times. After each shed they have a new flexible skin which permits further growth.

The caterpillar's appearance changes, too. On hatching it was light greyish-white with a shiny black head. In the later stages it is boldly striped with bands of black, white and yellow; these striking markings advertise that it is poisonous, packed as it is with cardiac glycosides derived from its food. As well as warning colours, the caterpillar has another method of defence. At both ends of its body the caterpillar has a pair of black filaments. The front ones, sometimes confused with antennae which no caterpillars have, are long and whip-like, while the ones at the rear are shorter and neater. These can be lashed through the air to startle or even club an attacker.

The caterpillar doesn't move around much. The antelope horn milkweed on which it grows is nearly 60 centimetres high with plenty of leaves, so it just has to move between meals, not between plants. All insects have three pairs of legs; caterpillars are no exception, although they seem to have more. The real ones are situated just behind their head, are equipped with small claws and are mainly used to grab leaves for eating. The soft and elongated bodies of caterpillars need extra support, so further back they have five pairs of appendages called pro legs. These are stubby, with hooks or crotchets to help the caterpillar cling and move along stems and leaves. They come into their own when the caterpillar pupates.

When searching for a suitable site for this next stage in its development it crawls, by caterpillar standards, fast and far. During this nomadic phase the surviving caterpillar travels over 70 metres to a small shrub, which it proceeds to climb. An infinite variety of objects that will give support and shelter may be selected as a pupation site – the underside of horizontal timbers of fences, eaves and windowsills of buildings, and the leaves of various plants, to name but a few. This caterpillar chooses to hang down from a twig at the top of the shrub. By attaching itself to the under-surface of an object, a pupa is shielded from both direct sunlight and rain.

The caterpillar spins a silk mat on to the twig and a button of silk on to the mat. Near its rear pair of pro legs are some hooks which it stabs into the silken button. Now secured, the caterpillar hangs down, with the front part of its body curved inwards to form a 'J' shape. It remains suspended for several hours before its final moult. The skin splits in the head region and the caterpillar wriggles, shakes and shivers to work it gradually backwards. Eventually the larval skin falls away, and the case of the pupa or chrysalis is revealed beneath. At first it's soft and milky green but the case hardens in an hour or so, becoming jade-green, with exquisite dots of silver and gold studding its surface. When the light strikes it a certain way, the whole structure shines with an intense metallic sheen.

This suspended capsule was once thought of as a resting stage, but this is far from the truth. Taking place inside is the climax of one of nature's most magical transformations. Surprisingly, the changes that give rise to the adult form were already quite well advanced inside the caterpillar. Most of a butterfly's familiar features – wings, antennae, compound eyes and proboscis – had differentiated from the tiny clusters of cells that carry the blueprint of the adult. (These cell clusters remain dormant in the caterpiller until just before pupation.)

The final stages of the ultimate in 'make-overs' take place inside the chrysalis. Our monarch's caterpillar can now be known as her daughter, as her eggs have already begun to develop. As well as a developing reproductive system, muscles are rejigged to be ready for powering flight. As the process draws to a close the pupal sheath clears, and bright orange wings can be seen folded inside. Precisely a month after our monarch had the near miss with the road cruiser and at about the same time she made a meal for a mantis, her daughter emerges from the chrysalis and is on the wing. She and other monarchs, the first-generation progeny of the butterflies that journeyed from Mexico, must now carry the baton and continue the colonization of a continent.

Like her mother before her, this monarch's priorities are to feed and mate. It isn't long before both her objectives are achieved. Flowering meadows provide nectar and are patrolled by newly emerged males which sally forth for any females that enter their air space. The early summer is warm and our female's eggs mature quickly. As she travels northwards, she unloads her ripe eggs on suitable milkweeds.

Her northward flight is swift and urgent – other than when roosting, she never stays in one place for longer than a few hours until she finds what for her is a paradise. Mason Neck wildlife refuge is on a finger of land jutting into the Potomac River about 30 kilometres from Washington DC. In early June, our monarch's daughter wends her way through a magnificent woodland of towering, century-old oaks and beeches with trunks a metre in diameter. She soars through a gap where the trees open out and finds herself overlooking a marsh with a cluster of shimmering pools. On the edge of these, with leafy stems well over a metre high, there are stands of swamp milkweed – enough fodder for hundreds of monarch caterpillars.

She glides low over the water and passes a tidy pile of branches plastered with mortar of mud and stones. The beaver lodge is divided into two parts: beneath the level of the water there is a food storage area, while the upper chamber with a ventilation hole at the top comprises the living quarters. Inside there is a female beaver with four kits. The adult, an example of the largest rodent in North America, weighs 27 kilograms. The babies, just a day old, weigh less than half a kilogram, but, remarkably, in a week they will be adept swimmers. Beavers are creators of wetland: behind their dams, rivers and streams overflow to create ponds and boggy land which can be perfect for swamp milkweed and hence for monarchs. Our butterfly flits between the plants and settles ten times to lay ten eggs.

She roosts in an alder tree high above the beaver dam. At first light, the wood-land is filled with the songs of birds which, like her, have a link with Mexico. Wood warblers are some of the most colourful of all North American birds, and many of them overwinter in Central America. Protonotary warblers spend the winter in the humid forests and mangroves of Mexico. Now a male sings from the top of the alder where the monarch rests. He repeats six to ten ringing 'swee' notes all on the same pitch. His grand name comes from the brilliant golden yellow of his head, throat and breast, which supposedly is a similar colour to that of the robes worn by papal clerks in ancient times. A distinctive rising buzzy song comes from a tall pine where a cerulean warbler proclaims his territory. Short-tailed and plump, he is blue above with black streaks and white wing bars. He spends the winter in South America in the foothills of the Andes. The magnolia warbler, which is now picking off tiny insects only 30 centimetres away from our monarch, doesn't travel as far. This black, yellow and white bird could very easily have migrated here from close to the magical Mexican forest where the monarch's mother's journey began. As the bird gleans for food, he knocks the monarch into flight.

The day is overcast but warm enough for the monarch to be active, and all around the beaver dam she deposits eggs on milkweeds. During a shower of rain she heads back up to the canopy where she's noticed by a blue jay. This wouldn't normally be a problem, but this blue jay has no experience of monarchs. A leaf screens the bird from the butterfly and with its head tilted to one side and crest slightly raised, the inquisitive jay edges closer. It cranes around the leaf and at last the monarch sees it. There is a flash of bright orange as the butterfly opens its wings. With its beady black eyes, the jay takes in the thick black veins, wide borders and large white dots on the orange wings. This pattern means nothing to the bird, but soon it will. The butterfly takes off and the jay plucks her out of the air with his gunmetal-grey bill. She isn't easy to swallow: her wings snag at the corners of the bird's beak, but eventually the inexperienced jay gulps her down. Two minutes later it coughs and chokes before vomiting up our monarch's body. The monarch's bright colours are a warning that the cardiac glycosides accumulated by the caterpillar are passed on to the adult. The bird will remember that eating these butterflies is an unpleasant experience and will leave them alone in the future. Unfortunately the lesson came too late for our monarch, but elsewhere the northward advance continues.

F ar to the north-west, the daughter of this monarch and granddaughter of the female that originally left Mexico sips nectar in a garden in Pittsburgh, Pennsylvania. She is just one of millions of summer monarchs originating from the butterflies that spent the previous winter in Mexico. Pittsburgh is a bustling steel city, but even in this conurbation there are milkweeds. In the northern USA, by far the most abundant species – as its name suggests – is the

A scarecrow is a silent witness as a banded golden spider partially paralyses a butterfly with a poisonous bite. The prey will then be totally immobilized by being ensheathed with silk

common milkweed. Unlike the antelope horn of Texas it has small flowers about half a centimetre wide, which are pink and clustered in dense umbels. Its leaves, however, are massive, up to 25 centimetres long and nearly 20 centimetres wide, while the plant itself can grow 2 metres tall.

The common milkweed can sustain the large population of monarchs in eastern North America, particularly here in the vicinity of the Great Lakes, because of its ability to grow in a wide variety of soil conditions. Our monarch's granddaughter negotiates the grid pattern of streets so common in American cities to lay eggs on plants on derelict ground, in a disused railway siding, on an abandoned basketball court, and even on a roof where a milkweed seed found enough soil in a crack to gain a precarious roothold.

It seems likely that human activity has caused the monarchs' migration path to move eastwards. The original centre of summer breeding was in the prairie states of the mid-west: the native grasslands boasted twenty-two milkweed species, as well as a diversity and abundance of other plants which provided a nectar bonanza for butterflies. First the steel plough, then combine harvesters pulled by twenty mules, led to the ruination of this magnificent habitat, and by 1910 most of the grasslands had been replaced with cornfields. In the north-east another pristine habitat was decimated, but ironically this boosted both milkweeds and monarchs.

By 1860 most of the north-eastern deciduous forest had been felled, and over the next thirty years, the remaining 200,000 square kilometres were cleared westward across the Great Lakes region. Shady woodland isn't ideal for common milkweed, but disturbed areas are. The plant made the most of these new opportunities and in consequence today it has become of overwhelming importance as a food-plant for monarchs.

Leaving Pittsburgh behind, the monarch comes to a hemlock swamp. Stands of huge old sugar maples tower above a meandering stream. Travelling along the bank, she flits over cinnamon, hay-scented, sensitive, Christmas and royal ferns. Nectar-rich blooms abound, and lazy flaps take her from one sun-lit feeding station to another.

As she unwinds her watch-spring proboscis, she registers a shape hurtling towards her. Although it can't resolve intricate patterns and shapes, the compound eye isn't inferior to the human one in every department. We cannot distinguish between more than about 20 events per second, but some insects can differentiate between 70 and 310 events per second. Their brains operate so fast that they can see in slow motion, which is why it is so difficult to swat a fly. To our eyes the wingbeats of a hummingbird are a continuous blur, but as the shape approaches and begins to feed on an adjacent flower the monarch can see individual flaps, even though the ruby-throated hummingbird's wings are beating 70 times a second.

The bird's wingspan of about 9 centimetres is the same as the monarch's, but flesh and feathers mean that it weighs just over three times as much – the butterfly is less than a gram. This bird is a male, with glittering crimson and green plumage. He hovers backwards from the flower and performs a courtship display for his drabber mate, who is perched nearby. His aerobatics are astonishing and he flies back and forth along the arc of a wide circle with swings so accurate and precise that he could be on a pendulum. His wings and tail emit a buzzing sound as he whizzes through the air. The monarch lifts off as he passes and has one last view of the hummingbird's throat with its crimson gorget flashing in the sunshine.

A fortnight later the butterfly approaches one of the continent's greatest spectacles. As she travels along a gorge the river below suddenly drops away. Even though her flightpath is high, drops of water from a curtain of suspended mist condense on her wings. Below, on the Niagara River, 3000 cubic metres of water a second (the equivalent of half a million full bath tubs) flow over a cataract which is 20 storeys high (85 per cent of the water at Niagara Falls plunges over these, the Horseshoe Falls). In spring, our monarch crossed over the Rio Grande into the United States; now her granddaughter crosses another river border, this time into Canada.

Pushing northwards, laying eggs en route, she reaches a patchwork of green and yellow just north of Toronto. The green patches are fields of ripening maize. The yellow component comes from sunflowers, their heads all facing into the sun. That night, as the monarch roosts, an elaborate snare is being constructed nearby. In front of a scarecrow silhouetted against the moon a silvered thread of silk floats through the air. The end of the thread catches on a twig and becomes taut, then begins to bounce as if a tightrope walker was doing back flips. A banded golden spider scurries part of the way along the thread and breaks it. Holding on to the broken end, the spider rolls it along in front of itself while reeling out a new thread behind. About halfway across the gap, the old and the new thread are connected, the spider then drops vertically with another silken line until it reaches a surface to fasten it to. This vertical thread pulls on the horizontal one to make it sag, and the resulting 'Y' structure is the basic framework of an orb web. Now the spider runs out twenty to thirty radial threads from the central hub. The angles between these radii are astonishingly constant, about 15 degrees. It seems that to measure this, the spider uses its front legs like compasses.

Now a spiral of silk can be interconnected with the radii. This auxiliary spiral is only a temporary structure which acts as a guide and scaffold for the laying of the sticky spiral. This is the spider's most difficult task. Working from the periphery, the spider crosses the radial threads in a spiral fashion, using both its front and hind legs to fasten the sticky thread to each radius. The auxiliary spiral is taken down as this construction proceeds. In under half an hour, the complex trap is complete. The moon is above the scarecrow's shoulder now, and the spider is illuminated in its cold light as it makes final adjustments in the central hub of its web.

There is a chill in the night air, the first sign of autumn, but at dawn the sun's disc blazes into a flawless sky, colouring drops of dew the same fiery orange as the monarch's wings. She is deep within a shrub waiting to be warmed into flight. The spider's gossamer snare is bejewelled with droplets of dew. When these burn off, the threads seem smooth, but a microscopic view shows there are still droplets resembling a string of pearl beads. These are not made of water but of liquid silk, the glue that gives the threads their holding power.

The monarch lifts off and begins to feed from flowers on the margin of a maize field. Butterflies, like other insects, can see ultra-violet light so in order to attract pollinators it pays for flowers to show up like beacons under these wavelengths. Many blooms also have ultra-violet marks to guide landing insects to their nectar. Ahead of our monarch, suspended in the vegetation, there are bright bars, crosses and a circle which strongly reflect ultra-violet light. She flutters to investigate and passes close to a scarecrow. The sunlight passing through its tattered straw hat is fractured into brilliant shards. Just as she reaches the ultra-violet pattern she collides with glutinous threads. A gust of wind blows through the scarecrow's innards of straw with a sibilant hiss.

The butterfly's struggles are to no avail as the spider's silk is super-strong. She has been duped; both the spider and the decorative silks in its web strongly reflect ultra-violet light, and this probably acts as a visual display to attract day-flying insects like her. The plump spider, which to our eyes is banded black and yellow, rushes towards our monarch's granddaughter. To partly paralyse the butterfly, it injects venom with one swift bite. To be totally immobilized, the victim must be wrapped in a silken shroud. Orb spiders have six glands, each producing a

Freshly emerged from its chrysalis, one of the autumn generation of monarchs dries its wings in Toronto. This fragile butterfly will soon begin a marathon flight to Mexico, 4000 kilometres away.

different type of silk. Shining strands are forced through nozzles on the spider's abdomen as it circles round and round its prey. The sheath of silk has another purpose as well — it conceals the food from wasps or birds that may pilfer from the web. Spiders don't seem to be deterred by monarch chemical defences and the body will be consumed, with the scarecrow as a silent witness.

Toronto is a bustling city. At the heart of this activity is Union Station, where weary commuters are now climbing on to trains to go home. On some waste ground, only a stone's throw away, a chrysalis hangs from a twig. A few hours ago the pupa became transparent; now furled orange wings can be seen inside. At dawn, one of our monarch's great-granddaughters will emerge.

The process begins when it's still pitch-dark. Along the sides of the pupa there is a line of tiny holes which open to the outside. Air is drawn in through these and swallowed by the butterfly inside. In this way she expands her body to split the pupal shell. As she rests the sun climbs above the canyons of steel and glass in the central business district, and three or four waves of commuters have already returned to the city. The butterfly uses her legs to widen the gap in the pupal shell and laboriously crawls out. She hangs down from the twig, as her crumpled wings begin to expand. To pump them up she again swallows air to increase her blood pressure. The fluid surging through the veins stretches and stiffens the wings which she dries in the sun. Her proboscis is as important as her wings and must be fitted together. It is composed of two halves, each concave on the inside, so that when the edges are joined together in a zipper-like arrangement they form a channel for imbibing nectar.

She hangs close to the ground, too close for comfort. As it darts forward to dispatch a beetle, a tiny hyperactive predator rustles a discarded candy bar wrapper below. The short-tailed shrew hunts ceaselessly to fuel its high-speed life and huge metabolic rate. It scents the monarch with its mobile snout. The insectivore's eyesight is poor, but it can make out the twitching orange form. It's not much bigger than the butterfly, but what it lacks in size it makes up for in ferocity. It leaps into the air and catches hold of a hind wing with its needle-sharp teeth. The butterfly flaps and labours skyward. The shrew drops back with a shred of wing in its jaw.

Our monarch's great-granddaughter will have this nick in her wing for life, the only imperfection in her beautiful construction, and as rising air from a thermal pushes against her wings, she gains elevation and soars effortlessly over a skyscraper. The Royal Bank of Canada is one of the tallest in the central business district and she is an orange speck against the vast expanse of mirrored glass. It is mid-September and this butterfly is part of the autumn generation, which is subtly different from the monarchs of the spring and summer. A state of reproductive diapause means that mating and egg-laying are on hold. Any food is used to build up fat reserves to fuel an incredible journey and tide them over the winter. Remarkably, a third of their body weight is made up of fat.

As she spirals south from Toronto, the newly emerged monarch arrives at a field of burnished yellow. There are hundreds of other monarchs feeding here: goldenrod is rich in nectar, which can now be converted into fat. Few milkweeds are in flower now but the leathery case of bear seedpods will break open along a well-defined fracture line when ripe. Inside, fluffy seeds are packed in rows like sardines, each with a parachute of down that will carry them away on the wind.

Many other plants have set seed or are in the process of doing so, and the woodlands are turning into a colourful tapestry. The leaves of aspen and birch are lime-green and gold, those of ash a smoky purple, while the maples are orange and red. Winter isn't far away, and the butterflies are in a race to stay ahead of the advancing frost.

Our monarch heads in a south-westerly direction and skirts the north shore of Lake Erie, looking for a place to cross. Along this flyway there are immense numbers of monarchs, travelling purposefully. In late afternoon they begin to funnel down a peninsula of land that juts into the lake. This is Point Pelee, a traditional stopping-place along the migratory pathway. Here this autumn generation show another behavioural difference: they assemble in trees and shrubs to sleep communally rather than roosting alone.

At dawn our monarch flexes her wings to catch the first warming rays of the rising sun. When she is warm enough for coordinated flight, she lifts off with a hundred others. Like autumn leaves they swirl down to sip nectar at a bank of purple New England oysters. The winds are favourable, so she doesn't feed for long, but she flutters aloft: the air stream carries her across the great sheet of water.

Continuing southwards, she flaps rather slowly, five to twelve times a second, but this still uses up valuable energy. Her fat reserves must last through the winter and get her started back north again in spring, so to clock up kilometres easily, this frail traveller is an expert at reading and riding the wind. She soars

OVERLEAF: *The flowers of goldenrod appear late in the year and are one of the most important sources of nectar for the monarchs. The butterflies use this food to build up fat reserves for travelling and to tide them over the winter.*

skywards on currents of warm air riding to altitudes of 7000 metres or more. Once there, she either glides long distances to earth (fixed-wing gliding uses perhaps 1 per cent of the energy of powered flight) or locates the high-altitude winds associated with northern cold fronts and rides them south. While waiting for the right winds, she stops to feed on nectar but never misses an opportunity to continue southwards. She falters in really cold weather but always travels if it's sunny and warm, even if the prevailing wind is a westerly. She lifts off and, like an experienced yachtsman, begins tacking, angling herself against the wind that blows towards the east in order to move herself south-west towards Mexico. Sometimes she expends little energy and the perfect wind can carry her 200 kilometres in a day.

This epic flight takes her over cities and villages, forests and meadows, mountains and deserts. She probably uses a whole range of navigational aids to find her way, a feat that is even more remarkable because she has never been to the destination before. On cloudless days her sun compass is probably most important, but when the sun is obscured another mechanism comes into play. Her brain contains minute crystals of magnetite, suggesting that she uses magnetic lines on the earth for orientation as well. This is probably only a back-up system for overcast days, because magnetic field lines are locally much more irregular and a less reliable source for direction than the sun.

By mid-October our monarch's great-granddaughter and a hundred million others funnel down through Texas before streaming out across Mexico's Sierra Madre mountains. But these ranges, running north and south, are not the ones they are looking for, so they continue their flight. By late autumn the millions of insects are approaching the trans-volcanic range of central Mexico. Long ago the volcanic forces fizzled and died; now the eroded cones have flattened tops and their sides are clothed with forests of fir and pine. At an altitude of some 3400 metres there is a glade surrounded by oyamel pines which, about seven months ago, our original monarch left to start her journey. Now her great-granddaughter will overwinter amongst the same trees.

Monarchs congregate here and in eleven similar sites nearby for a number of reasons. They are basically tropical butterflies and freezing temperatures are fatal to eggs, larvae, chrysalises and adults, so they don't have the option of brazening out the winter in North America. An overwintering site must be warm, but not so hot that the monarchs burn up their fat supply; moist enough to prevent desiccation; and protected enough to avoid freezing air and heavy snows. The groves provide all these requirements and are also unbeatable for perches: the broad leaves of deciduous trees could not support such immense numbers of butterflies

– the hollow pine needles are easier to grasp and have footholds that are closer together so the insects can cram more tightly in. By clustering together the monarchs conserve the small amount of heat produced by their bodies. This accumulates in a gathering of a million insects, and the centre of the cluster is warmer than the surrounding air. The forest of oyamel pine is not a paradise though – here there is lethal danger too.

In mid-November our monarch is dormant and clings to the bark of a vertical trunk. With thousands of other butterflies packed so closely, it is impossible to see the tree beneath. The night has been cold and their wings are tightly closed. The gloomy dawn is brightened by a dazzling red bird with cheeks of silver-grey. The aptly named red warbler lives in these mountains all year round, and is rarely found below 2000 metres and never outside Mexico. It searches for hibernating insects, lifting and pulling back leaves as if playing peek-a-boo. Monarchs are too large to be of interest to the warbler, but there are two kinds of birds which, during the winter, feed on virtually nothing else. During the overwintering period in one colony of 23 million monarchs, they were estimated to have killed over two million.

The colourful marauders come in a mixed flock of some thirty birds. They swoop through the forest to alight on our monarch's tree. At first they remain still and just look at the tropical butterflies, as if spoilt for choice. A black-headed oriole attacks first. As it daintily plucks at a monarch, a cascade of others fall to the ground. Its victim feebly opens its wings, a flash of orange against the bird's bright yellow chest. The oriole then holds the insect under its scaled foot and, with some nifty beakwork, strips out the fleshy insides of the abdomen, discarding the wings and cuticle.

Dislodged monarchs rain down from all over the tree as more birds begin to attack. The duller female orioles, more olive than yellow, process the insects in the same way. They've learnt that even small amounts of monarch poison make them vomit, so they only eat parts of the body free of cardiac glycosides. Our monarch nearly falls as a second species of bird flaps past to pick off one of her neighbours. The black-headed grosbeak is stockier than the orioles, with a much chunkier beak. He lands on a nearby branch in a flurry of cinnamon, black and brown; his mate is brown with dark streaks and a creamy-white eyebrow and stripe on the crown. Unlike orioles, grosbeaks can consume monarch toxins with no ill effects – with a flick of his head he twists off the insect's wings and swallows the body whole.

Cold monarchs lie on the ground all around but there is safety in numbers: the butterflies on the periphery of the cluster are most at risk. Our monarch still grasps the bark.

In Mexico there are eleven overwintering sites with around 14 million monarchs per hectare. Basking butterflies carpet the forest floor; to return to their roost they must fly or climb into the trees. At night grounded butterflies may be killed by frosts or predatory mice.

The oyamel pines disappear under a covering of orange insects. It's advantageous for a monarch to be in the centre of a cluster. It is not as warm on the periphery and butterflies there are more likely to be attacked by birds.

The depredations of the bird skims off some of the monarchs every winter but this year the butterflies must endure an event that is much rarer. One day in January fluorescent clouds coalesce and the sky turns steely grey. Then snowflakes begin to fall, slowly at first and then in dense, swirling clouds; inexorably the snow begins to settle on the ground and in the trees.

On the vertical trunk our monarch isn't in direct contact with the freezing blanket, but above there is an ominous cracking sound. Due to the combined weight of snow and butterflies a branch snaps. As it crashes to the ground, it sweeps down the trunk dislodging any butterflies in its path. Our monarch falls. More than 10,000 butterflies are either crushed instantly or trapped hopelessly by the branch, but our monarch is thrown to one side. She lies still in a carpet of torpid butterflies which soon have a thin covering of snow. The fallen monarchs could be killed by freezing ground temperatures or eaten by a predator that stalks them at night.

In the afternoon watery sunshine filters through the trees, but it hasn't enough power to warm the stranded monarchs into flight. Water from the melting snow trickles between their wings, which begin to vibrate. At dusk our monarch is part of a fiery patch. Shivering is the butterflies' best chance of escape. In this way they may be able to warm up their muscles just enough to scramble to safety.

In the gathering darkness, our monarch begins to walk. Her feet barely touch the ground as she crawls over the papery wings of the dead and dying. Other survivors also crawl laboriously, searching for anything to climb. Suddenly one is yanked backwards into a ground-hugging plant. Behind the foliage, the insect's innards and muscles are stripped out. The black-eared mouse then drags her spoils between some roots and down into a burrow. A litter of nearly weaned babies squabble over the food. This is the only mouse to feed extensively on monarchs; it tries to avoid their toxins but it can tolerate them if it has to. It even times its breeding period to coincide with the butterflies' overwintering period.

The mouse, almost a caricature with silvery whiskers, bulging eyes and translucent ears, scurries out of her burrow once more. As she runs over butterfly wings, her skittering feet sound as if they're on tissue paper. A movement attracts her and she darts forward to sink her teeth into another victim. Nearly a metre above, our monarch climbs higher, and soon she settles back amongst butterflies clustered on the trunk. Snow is not an annual event here and a heavy fall such as this takes a terrible toll — some 20 per cent of the overwintering monarchs are killed.

There is little chance of the monarch as a species becoming extinct. Farther south in Central America, smaller populations are active all year and migrants blown off course have founded new colonies in Australia and southern Europe, but it's only the North American populations that aggregate in awe-inspiring numbers. East of the Rocky Mountains and Great Plains, hundreds of millions of butterflies coalesce into eleven sites near the centre of Mexico. In the chosen groves there are a staggering fouteen to fifteen million butterflies per hectare. In 1983 conservationists decided the North American populations that migrated and overwintered here in Mexico and in California had become the first example of a 'threatened phenomenon'.

With this recognition it is hoped that the sites will remain safe, but there is still cause for concern. In Mexico the oyamel fir is a valuable timber resource, while coastal land in California (where the monarchs from the western United States overwinter) is a prime target for resort development. Only 150-200 square miles of high-altitude oyamel fir forests, so crucial to overwintering monarchs, are left in all of Mexico and their piecemeal destruction continues. The trees must be preserved to avoid a catastrophe.

The monarch phenomenon is at its most extraordinary in the spring, when rising temperatures stimulate the butterflies to find their wings. They fill the skies from just above the ground to the height of the tallest pines. When the sun shines through their wings, the butterflies become a luminous orange and, as they flutter and glide, they trace ever-changing kaleidoscopic patterns in the sky.

One day in late February, our original monarch's great-granddaughter forms part of a dazzling parade that pours through the pine glades to a stream. She sails in to land on some damp mud with a flotilla of other butterflies. Here she unfurls her proboscis and uses it as a flexible drinking straw to replace some of the moisture lost while she has been hanging in the tree.

The rising temperatures have also activated her reproductive system, and as she flutters up she joins a cloud of mating butterflies. Now she has sperm to fertilize her eggs and an energy implant for their growth and the journey ahead. Just like her great-grandmother last year, she will head northwards soon to begin a new colonization of the United States. This is the first leg of an annual odyssey that is unique in the animal kingdom. Monarchs have evolved this remarkable migration to exploit the milkweeds of North America. By the end of the summer several generations will have been born, bred and died before the final generation reaches as far north as Canada. These monarchs of autumn then fly over 4000 kilometres on a route and to a destination of which they have no direct knowledge. The fact that these travellers seem so frail makes this feat even more astounding. It is difficult to believe that this journey is real, and not just a flight of fancy.

The desert forms a backdrop as a grey whale breaches or leaps right out of the water in a Mexican breeding lagoon.

5

THE WHALE'S VOYAGE

ATHED IN THE warm waters of a sub-tropical lagoon there is a brand new baby. A baby that weighs 900 kilograms and is 4 metres long. Like her mother and all grey whales (*Eschrichtius robustus*), the calf is destined to spend her life travelling. If she survives for forty years she will cover a distance equivalent to going to the moon and back. Every year she will attempt an epic round trip of more than 16,000 kilometres. This incredible journey spans three seas and will take her up and down nearly the whole of the Pacific coast of North America.

The breeding grounds are in Mexican waters, so now the whales are at the most southerly point of their ocean odyssey. The newborn calf is in the San Ignacio lagoon, an embayment on the west coast of Baja California, that skinny finger of land extending into the North Pacific, south from the border of the United States. It's January, the peak time for births, so the lagoon contains about 100 mothers and calves, together with over 250 single grey whales, bulls and cows without young. The calf spends the first day of her life in the seclusion and calm of the innermost portion of the lagoon, in water less than 4 metres deep.

She can't cope with currents or choppy water, and finds it a strain to coordinate her un-cooperative mass of muscles. Even movements that will become second nature are difficult at first. For instance, she doesn't need to toss her whole head out of the water to take a breath. On top of her head directly above her eyes are a pair of blowholes that are, in fact, nostrils, As she becomes experienced she simply breaks the surface with them to breathe smoothly and efficiently, even when travelling at speed.

The calf has smooth dark skin which is still creased from where she was curled up inside her mother's uterus. Her flippers are flaccid and rubbery, so her first attempts at swimming are erratic and she never ventures far. For much of the time she is either cradled by her mother's massive flippers or rides on her vast back.

When observed at the surface the cow is like an iceberg – only the tip can be seen. But from under the water, even though the visibility is poor, the calf can see what she herself will look like if she reaches adulthood. Her mother's body stretches into the distance – at 12 metres she's a shade longer than a bus. Her weight is 30 tonnes, equivalent to that of ten good-sized elephants. Instead of a dorsal fin she has a hump two-thirds of the way along her back and ten smaller bumps or knuckles scattered along her tail. Her eyes, the size of oranges, are 2.5 metres back from the tip of her snout. As the calf moves in the swell she feels that her mother's body isn't as smooth as her own – the roughness of the charcoal-grey skin is caused by clusters of encrusted barnacles. Others like these will soon colonize the baby whale and her skin won't be pristine for long.

The calf grows rapidly, nourished on milk that is 50 per cent fat – about 15 times the percentage of fat found in milk from a dairy cow. She guzzles over 200 litres of this rich liquid every single day, suckling it from nipples recessed in shallow folds on her mother's lower belly. Until the calf becomes proficient at swimming, mother and baby keep mostly to themselves. When the calf is a few days old they leave the sheltered waters of the inner lagoon and join other cows and calves in a sort of playgroup. The calves find the cows as entertaining as a water park. They use their mothers' broad backs as slides, rolling on to them before gliding off in a watery glissade. An exhalation from a mother's blowhole makes a perfect jacuzzi. When they play together, groups of calves unwittingly practise the skills they'll need in the future. They can now swim on a steady course, but they'll need stamina on the long journey to come. For endurance training, the calf joins a phalanx of other youngsters swimming into the powerful currents that surge through the entrance of the lagoon. When they tire of the aquatic treadmill one calf sneaks up to splash another by slapping the water surface with its flippers. For now this is a game, but in the perilous months ahead it could save their lives. The calf feels the caress of her mother's flipper drawing her alongside: it's time to return to the sanctuary of the inner lagoon.

The whales don't have exclusive use of these waters and the calf encounters other birds and animals, some of which are as playful as she. Sunset at the end of a glorious sub-tropical day turns the water into a rippling sheet of orange silk. Fish dance in the shallows right next to the calf until a dozen projectiles of brown and red scatter the shoal: she watches as the brown pelicans dive into the school of fish. The birds have bright pink pouches under their throats which they use as fleshy landing nets. Once their heads are above the surface, it takes the birds up to a minute to drain 10 litres of water from their pouches and to eat the fish trapped inside. The pelicans soon have bulging crops of food for their young. As they head for their nesting colony on a nearby island, they skim low over the waves and the whales in single file.

Within seconds other projectiles arrive – this time to play not to feed. At almost 4 metres, the bottle-nosed dolphins are nearly as long as the calf. She rolls on her mother's back to watch curiously as the grey and white dolphins repeatedly explode into the air. Liquid orange streams off their glistening bodies as a deluge of falling water takes on the colour of the setting sun. At the end of each arcing dive, their heads cleave the surface of the lagoon and they disappear beneath, before erupting skywards once more.

As the grey whales move off, the dolphins ride the pressure wave of the cow and cavort even closer to the calf. The procession of dolphins and whales crosses the lagoon in the twilight.

The mother and calf sleep just below the surface. Every ten minutes or so they languidly rise for breaths of air. As she rests, the calf's smooth skin is colonized by a cargo of hitch-hikers. When newborn whales are around some creatures fill the lagoon with microscopic larvae. As these larvae float into contact

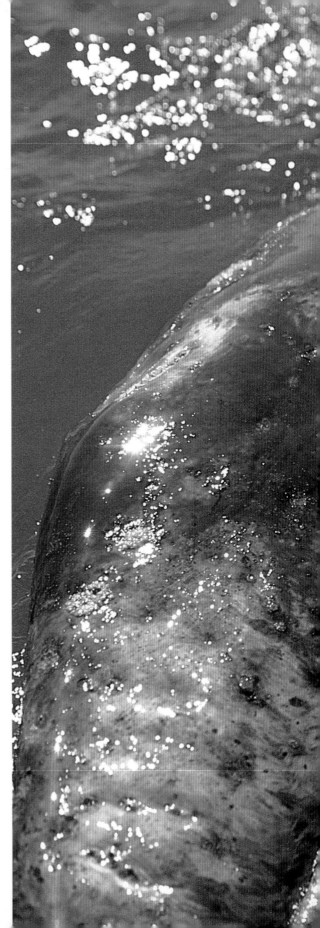

Newborn whales have smooth grey skin. This will soon be colonized by the larvae of barnacles which are abundant in the waters of the breeding lagoon. The clusters of crustaceans will form tough whitish blotches, particularly around the whale's head.

The 2.4 centimetre long whale lice which infest a grey whale's skin seem like creatures from a nightmare. In fact they perform a useful service in cleaning up wounds and flakes of dead skin.

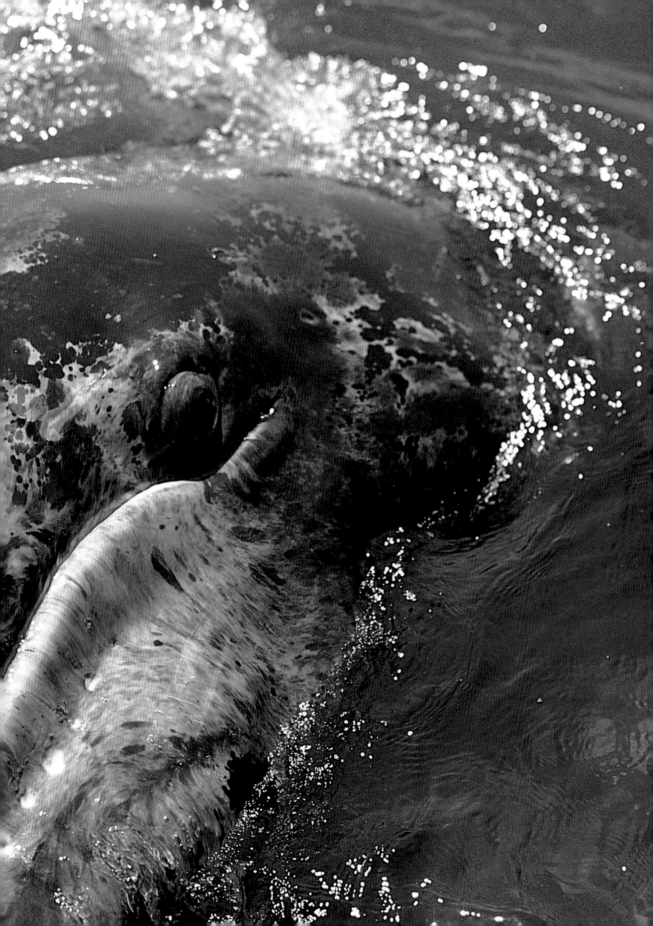

with the calf's skin they grip and walk over the surface, using sticky pads on the curved antennae-like structures protruding from their heads. They find a suitable site and cement themselves into position; they will never move by their own devices again. Soon they'll grow a ring of overlapping limestone plates, which act as both armour and anchor. The base of the protective shells of whale barnacles penetrates the skin of their host, so they can't easily be dislodged. This species of barnacle attaches itself exclusively to grey whales, and eventually the calf will have solid white colonies on her head, flippers, back and tail flukes. These barnacles have an easier life than the more familiar species that attach themselves to rocks on the beach. Those have to beat their six pairs of feathery legs to waft food into their mouths; whale barnacles merely have to wait for the movement of their transporter to bring food within reach. Like fouling organisms on the hull of a boat these 'hangers-on' can increase the drag on a swimming whale, but other than this the barnacles won't cause the calf any harm.

A coyote's howl carries across the lagoon from the desert. As she rocks gently next to her mother, other hitch-hikers climb on to the calf . The ebb and flow of the moonlit swell reveals sinister, pale creatures about 2 centimetres long. They scuttle along on five pairs of legs to transfer from mother to baby, and then head for a secure refuge. Some cling with powerful pincers to the inside of the calf's blowholes, while others choose the grooves on her throat. They're called whale lice, but are not really lice at all – in fact they are amphipods, which belong to the same group as the sandhoppers found on the strandline. Three different species spend their lives on grey whales; indeed, two of them are found nowhere else. They can be extremely abundant – one individual grey is known to have carried more than 100,000 of them. For these lice, a grey whale provides food (the amphipods scavenge on old flaky skin and any damaged tissues) as well as being a convenient means of transport. Now that these colonists have settled on the body of the calf they will accompany her on her great natural journey, although some of them won't even make it out of the lagoon.

At dawn a school of silvery fish come to groom the whales. The top smelt cleaning service is free, and they flash in and out to pick off flakes of old skin. They also snaffle up barnacles and whale lice that are not attached securely. This extra food is protein-rich and supplements the top smelts' more usual diet of marine plants.

The lagoon is not always so idyllic. A tropical storm, the Chubuscos, can surge up from the south. Skies of perfect blue become a dull grey and the backs of surfacing whales lose their shine. The wind whips up white horses and stirs up sediment, reducing visibility to less than 25 centimetres. The contrast between the whales' world and the transparent one of the creatures of the land is never greater than now. In fact, there are few opportunities on the migration route for a grey to see much more than a whale-length ahead. Hearing is more important than vision in seas such as these. Water is much better than air at transmitting sounds, which can sometimes echo through hundreds of kilometres. During a storm the mother and calf, who is now a month old, venture into deeper water. They produce a repertoire of grunts, metallic knocks, tonal moans and other sounds like the metallic ring of Caribbean steel drums. Their voices are primarily for keeping in contact with each other; greys don't have the elaborate sonar of the other whales and dolphins, although they may use some low-frequency sounds as a primitive sonar to determine their relative depth in shallow seas.

There's a reverberation in the water ahead. The calf's mother has heard this moan before and she turns her baby away. Two males are competing for a female, and the calf could be injured if she approaches too closely. Her mother also wants to avoid the attention of the bulls – she won't mate while she's caring for a baby. Next spring, when the calf is independent, she'll become receptive again. The gestation period of grey whales is twelve to thirteen months, so most cows give birth every two years. The bulls are in pursuit of a mature cow who is in breeding condition. During the high-speed chase their mighty tail flukes churn and slap the brown water into foam. Eventually the cow slows down, signalling her willingness to mate. Gently the bulls caress her with their flippers. Then she rolls on her side so that one of the males can copulate with her. The unsuccessful bull will have other opportunities. Grey whales are promiscuous and over the course of a breeding season, both sexes appear to mate with several partners.

The mother and calf are now 1.5 kilometres away but through the water they can still hear the successful bull as he blasts bubbles through his blowhole. The inquisitive calf is in shallow water; by resting her tail flukes on the bottom she can stand vertically, so that her head and eyes are out of the water. To look round she slowly turns through 180 degrees. This is the first time she's 'spy-hopped', a characteristic part of grey whale behaviour. She can see well in the air and she surveys San Ignacio: the lagoon is surrounded by the Vizcaino Desert, a stark landscape of searing white saltflats, while the horizon is punctured by giant cardon cacti. As the calf turns seawards she can see the line of breakers marking the inlet of the lagoon; she and her mother will soon negotiate them on the start of their northward trek.

While the calf makes the most of her new skill she sees evidence of other grey whales. When they breathe out an explosive cloud of spray emerges from their blowholes, sometimes reaching as high as 4 metres. The whales are blowing out foul air, not water – droplets of condensation form when relatively warm air from their lungs comes into contact with cooler air above the sea. The spout may be made more visible by droplets of mucous oil from the lungs, expelled during the coughing action of the blow. As the calf slowly turns there are bush-shaped blows all over the lagoon. When her mother takes a breath she gets a close-up view. No wind deflects the tiny droplets and the spout, characteristically for grey whales, is in the shape of a heart. The sun has returned and a perfect miniature rainbow curves through the spray. The delicate drops land on the calf's head as she sinks back down.

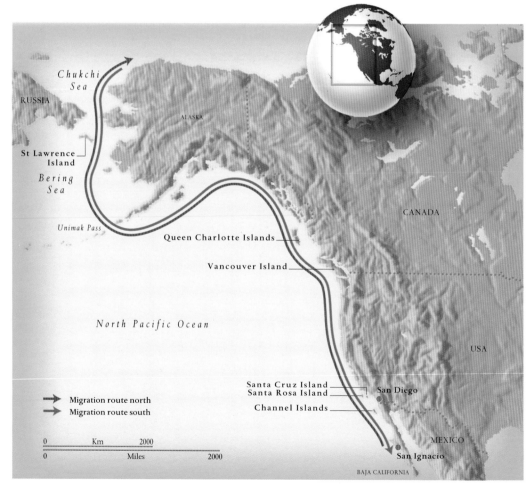

Chukchi Sea

RUSSIA

ALASKA

St Lawrence Island

Bering Sea

Unimak Pass

Queen Charlotte Islands

Vancouver Island

CANADA

North Pacific Ocean

USA

Santa Cruz Island
Santa Rosa Island
Channel Islands

San Diego

→ Migration route north
→ Migration route south

0   Km   2000
0   Miles   2000

MEXICO

San Ignacio

BAJA CALIFORNIA

It's mid-March, and only cows with young remain at San Ignacio. Newly impregnated cows, bulls and immature whales left the lagoon a month ago in the first pulse of the northward migration. Now it's the turn of the new mothers and calves. As her mother negotiates the sandbars at the mouth of the lagoon, our calf stays close. They're in a shallow channel which opens out into the North Pacific. Our calf has never seen water as blue and transparent as this. Other animals join them as they leave the inlet – chocolate-brown creatures which contort their bodies into the most complex geometric shapes. The calf watches as the Californian sealions dive beneath the waves and ascend to chase their own silvery bubbles. Her mother calls and the calf catches up: they must leave the sealions and sub-tropics behind.

Heading north along the Mexican coast, the cow swims with determination. In these waters there is

On migration grey whales often swim in formation just below the surface. They can travel at 7 kilometres per hour and cover 160 kilometres in a day, although mothers with young calves move at a slower pace.

little food, and she has lost 40 per cent of her body weight. To replenish her reserves she must journey with her calf to Arctic seas.

To propel themselves forward the whales beat their tail flukes up and down. Their streamlined bodies are designed to ease movement through the water. Any protuberances that would increase drag have been lost: even a neck and shoulders are missing, and their elongated heads merge smoothly with their bodies. So that nothing breaks the flow of water over their bodies, the whales' ears are reduced to two tiny openings on the side of their heads. Even their teats are hidden in slits.

But, even with this superb design, the calf tires easily. To save energy she travels just behind her mother's mid-section, as the water passing between the two of them helps pull her along. She's now perfected the art of breathing at speed, and just breaks the surface with her blowholes. These have a direct link to her lungs, so even with a mouthful of water she won't miss a breath. When she's travelling underwater, which on migration takes place for three to five minutes at a time, the blowholes are closed by a valve. After a week at sea the calf can cover 160 kilometres in a day, at speeds of up to 7 kilometres per hour.

For the most part our two whales travel alone, but sometimes they join other cows and their calves. San Ignacio is just one of four breeding lagoons along the coast of Baja California and all of the new mothers with babies in tow are now journeying northwards. Travelling alongside her mother, our calf learns the route. She tastes the chemical signature of the river systems and estuaries that they pass, so she'll recognize them again. The water is too deep to spy-hop by planting her flukes on the bottom, so she extends her head vertically from the sea by using rapid thrusts of her tail. In this way she can scan the coastline for visual landmarks for thirty seconds or more. She also hears her way and listens to the surf pounding on the shore. If she simply keeps this sound on her right side she's sure to be travelling in the right direction.

For much of the time the whales can use these basic methods of navigation, as their migratory route is rarely more than a few kilometres offshore. In only a few days the calf and her mother have travelled many kilometres and are near the Californian city of San Diego. The calf is fortunate to get this far – over a third of the grey whales born each year fail to leave Mexican waters. In the breeding lagoons weak calves can become stranded on sandbars and sandbanks, while in the open sea others lose contact with their mothers and fall easy prey to sharks.

The two whales spend the night in a sheltered bay so that the calf can nurse and rest. The water is slightly cooler here and the inshore waters are dominated by tangled forests of giant kelp, a seaweed with strap-like fronds which can grow to 10 metres in length. At dawn there is a cacophony of sound – an uproar of harsh froggy croaks, clucks and staccato clicks against a background of soft drumming. The kelp forest is home to an orchestra of fish and shrimps. Pistol shrimps live either in natural burrows or retreats or in ones they've constructed themselves. One species, *Alpheus pachychirus*, makes a sleeping bag out of a mat of algae. Using one of its slender pointed legs as a needle and algal filaments as thread, it stitches the mat together and pulls it around itself like a cloak. Since birth, and particularly now she is in the kelp forest, our whale calf has always been within earshot of these shrimps. They have specialized front claws for sound production – a movable upper finger with a part that fits into the socket of a lower movable one. The pistol is cocked when the two claws are held apart by adhesive discs, but when this force is broken by a muscular contraction the claw closes forcefully, generating a snapping or popping noise and a tiny jet of water. The shrimps use this trick to deter predators, to advertise for mates and when in a dispute over territory or food.

The dawn chorus of fish takes place for the same reasons that birds sing – to proclaim a territory and attract a mate. Drum fish, black spot fin and yellow fin croakers have special muscles to twitch their swim bladders, which vibrate to produce sounds. The sound system of the toad fish is so good that its calls are as noisy as a riveting machine or a subway train. The calf floats close to another player, a male garibaldi who is trying to entice females to lay eggs in his nest, a carpet of cropped algae on a rock wall. The fiery orange fish performs somersaults, making a clucking sound with every revolution. He interrupts the dance when he sees the whale's monstrous eye looming above and dives for a crevice. Remembering these subtle sounds pinpoints the calf's position on the migration route.

As well as these natural sounds, the calf and her mother have to endure the racket made by humans and their developments. For most of the migration route the greys must compete with people for coastal habitat. As the calf spy-hops to scrutinize landmarks she sees ships and skyscrapers, even the twisted metal form of a giant roller-coaster. It may be because many of the greys can't tolerate the increase in ship traffic and noise levels that in recent times the course of their migration has changed. Instead of hugging the southern Californian shoreline, the calf and her mother veer away and for the first time swim over deep water, out of sight of land.

The whales are heading for St Margaret, one of California's channel islands. They must now read the map provided by the earth's geomagnetic field, because there are no permanent landmarks here – anything solid either floats or swims. The calf and her mother approach a drifting mat of kelp, torn by a winter gale from the forest fringing the shore. There are invertebrates hidden in the tangle, and these have attracted some extraordinary ocean wanderers.

A group of molas or giant ocean sunfish is sprinkled with light diffracted by the waving fronds. Bizarre apparitions, they seem to be swimming heads because their bodies are nearly circular, as deep as they are long; up to 3 metres in diameter. Lacking a true tail, these fish propel themselves with long fins, one above and one below their massive bodies, which can weigh up to 2.5 tonnes. They look like millstones, which is what 'mola' means in Latin. The calf sees one of the creatures peel off from the others and ascend gracefully to the surface, twisting over to expose the flipside of its body to the sun. This basking behaviour gave ocean sunfish their English name. It's thought that molas rest on their side at the surface to warm up their bodies and speed up the digestion of their food. They are no threat to the whales as they eat small fish, squid, crustaceans and gelatinous

In a courtship frenzy, a trio of grey whales churn the waters of San Ignacio lagoon. A cow has two ardent suitors. One prepares to mate, his penis a metre long and almost 35 centimetres in diametre.

plankton; jellyfish are their favourite food. Unlike the whales, it seems that these mysterious fish are nomads rather than migrants. As long as the water isn't too cold, they can turn up anywhere.

As the mother and calf swim over a deep canyon, a huge shape soars to the surface. The baby moves closer to her mother but relaxes when the cow shows no sign of panic and doesn't call in alarm. The leviathan ahead is the largest creature ever to have inhabited the planet. Greys are mid-sized whales; seven other species are more massive. This blue whale is the biggest of them all: it is nearly 30 metres long and weighs 150 tonnes. As it breaks the surface to breathe the calf can see that its back is a pale, bluish-grey mottled with dingy white, while its creamy underside has patches of mustard yellow. These bright splashes are a film of diatoms, microscopic plants which travel the oceans on the belly of the blue, taking in nutrients from the sea and trapping energy from the sun. The whale sustains its huge body by gulping in sea water and fil-tering out krill, tiny shrimp-like creatures. These deep coastal canyons are the blue whales' summer home, but the greys' is still far to the north.

As they meander through the channel islands our calf's mother eats her first meal since leaving north-

A grey whale 'spy-hops' for a good look around. In this instance the coastal waters are shallow enough and the whale raises its head by planting its tail firmly on the bottom.

ern waters many months before. Myriads of dancing translucent shrimps shimmer in the sunlit waters. Opening her mouth, the cow lunges straight through the shoal. Like the blue and all other baleen whales, she has a curtain of stiff hairs hanging down from each side of her upper jaw instead of teeth. This baleen acts like a sieve, trapping the shrimps as sea water is forced out through the sides of her mouth. Our calf copies her mother. It takes her a few attempts to learn this lunge-feeding technique but eventually she tastes solid food for the first time. A start has been made on the long process of weaning, which won't be completed until our whales are in Arctic seas. As well as shrimps, the cow and her calf also gulp down a few mouthfuls of anchovies. These are insignificant meals for the adult who still relies on the fat reserves she accumulated in the feeding grounds the previous summer. Blue and all other baleen whales feed almost exclusively like this but this isn't the grey's preferred method of feeding. They use their unique foraging technique in the latter stages of their northward trek.

Once again the mother and her calf head for inshore waters. The two whales pass along the coasts of Oregon and Washington state, covering 150 kilometres in a day. Their nemesis waits for them as they enter Canadian waters. It is midday, and the calf is nursing at the mouth of a bay. The only sounds are her slurps, the odd click of a pistol shrimp and the susurrating sound of wave action shifting pebbles on a shingle beach. Unbeknown to the greys, a jet-black fin is slicing through the water towards them. In the shape of an isosceles triangle, it's some 2 metres high and belongs to a male orca or killer whale. There are two distinct forms of this superlative predator. 'Residents' live in extended family groups or pods of between five and twenty-five animals. They rarely stay underwater for more than four minutes, constantly chatter amongst themselves and feed mainly on fish such as salmon. The other type are 'transients' which live in pods of between one and seven, stay submerged for between five and fifteen minutes at a time and vocalize rarely, particularly when they want to surprise the large warm-blooded prey on which they specialize. Six of these killers bear down on the unsuspecting greys in a cloak of silence.

Our calf's mother swivels at the surface just in time – the orcas are nearly upon them. Now that they have been discovered the hunters produce bursts of ear-splitting ultrasonic sound. The mother grey cries in alarm to her petrified calf. The orcas are dwarfed by the adult grey – they're not much bigger than the calf, who has grown to 8 metres long. The sleek predators must hunt cooperatively to tackle outsized prey like this.

The male orca launches the initial attack. With a tremendous burst of speed he rakes his teeth along the tail fluke of the cow. She lifts her 4-metre tail into the air and spins the killer away. The old whalers didn't call greys 'devil fish' for nothing – they are a dangerous adversary when enraged and protecting young. As the mother and calf head shorewards, the killers zigzag across their path. An adult female orca makes another parry. Moving at more than 50 kilometres per hour, she's a blur of jet-black and brilliant white. As the killer opens her jaws, revealing a vivid pink and white mouth, our calf's mother lifts the baby out of the water on her flipper. Another voracious killer hurtles in from the other side. Its teeth graze the cow's grey skin and scrape off a layer of barnacles. The mother gently places her baby back into the water before ramming the killer with her head. 'Hard head' was another nickname given to greys by the old whalers. The calf makes good use of a skill she practised in the breeding lagoon: a lunging orca veers away as she smashes down her flipper right in front of its nose. But the relentless attack continues.

In open water the greys have little chance. Working as a team, the orcas lunge in turn. Time after time they force the larger whale to slash with her tail flukes or hit out with her head. The killers' strategy is to chase their victims to exhaustion, like hunting dogs running down their prey on the African plains. The greys plough through a forest of kelp. Something scrapes the underside of the calf, but it's a sharp rock, not the teeth of an orca. The mother and her youngster are in shallow water and, enveloped in kelp, they lose sight of their pursuers, and the seaweed muffles the hunters' ultrasonic calls. Tired and bloody, the mother grey lifts her massive head above the waves. There is a semi-circle of jet-black fins at the edge of the kelp, then she sees the killers break formation, turn and head back out to sea.

The pod broke off its attack because orcas are hesitant about entering dense stands of seaweed, probably because the fronds interfere with their sonar. The grey drops back down through the cloying, but life-saving, kelp. If she hadn't found refuge here the orcas would now be feasting on her tongue and throat blubber. After they'd eaten these, a delicacy to them, they may have discarded the rest of her body. Today there was a different outcome and neither the mother nor the calf has serious injuries. Their flesh wounds are soon pale orange, plastered with a seething mass of whale lice which scuttle in quickly to feed. Unwholesome as this may sound, the lice clear the lacerations of damaged tissue and are probably beneficial. The calf will bear witness to the sharpness of killer whale teeth for the rest of her life: on her tail fluke there will be a set of long, parallel, pure white scars.

When they are hunted by killer whales, greys may seek refuge in forests of kelp. The killers stay on the periphery of the dense strands of seaweed as it interferes with their sonar.

When mature, killer whale bulls have a 2 metre dorsal fin (double the size of a cow's). These predators work as a coordinated team to hunt down the much larger greys.

A killer may only eat the tongue and throat blubber from a grey whale carcass, ignoring the rest. This grey had a narrow excape – the white scars on its tail fluke are the tooth marks of a killer.

After resting for a few hours, the grey whales continue their journey and at dawn the next day they reach Vancouver Island. It's early May, and most of the western Pacific's population of greys have already travelled past the island. In April, at the peak passage, 200 went by in a day. The only grey whales here now are stragglers and a few individuals who aren't trekking farther north. This is because the waters here are rich in certain kinds of shrimp which can support a few greys all summer long. But mothers with young calves need super-abundant food for growth and for building fat reserves, which only Arctic waters can provide.

As they pass along the coastline the mother and calf hear the thrum of a flotilla of boats. One after another they accompany the whales, never impeding their progress and never getting too close. On the decks whale-watchers whoop excitedly, and the calf sees flashes of bright light as binoculars are lifted in the sun. The calf can't know, but as a grey whale she is the people's whale. The propensity of her species to travel so close to shore makes them accessible to humans. Today's whale-watchers care about the survival of grey whales, and they're the ones whose voices will be raised if the ancestral migration route is polluted with oil, impacted with industry or blocked by lethal nets. This hasn't always been the case, but the ships that came to the ancestors of our calf carried passengers who cared little about the future of the greys. These people didn't come to watch and wonder, but to chase and kill.

Shore whaling began in 1854, and grey whales were intercepted on their migratory route for the next forty-five years. Each whale taken yielded twenty-five to forty-five barrels of oil, which in 1855 sold at between $27 and $40 a barrel. The Baja breeding grounds were discovered in 1845: and at its peak, the devastation saw on average of 486 kills a year. By 1874 the records showed that about 8100 whales had lost their lives. Mortally wounded animals that managed to escape were not included in this figure, so it's an underestimate of the true slaughter. The whalers paid no attention to the fact that in the breeding lagoons they were killing the population's future: females and their young. They even injured calves solely for the purpose of drawing the enraged mothers within range of their harpoons. The butchery reduced numbers so considerably that by the end of the nineteenth century whaling for greys had become uneconomic and was largely abandoned. In spite of this wholesale slaughter about 4000 whales survived into the twentieth century.

The whalers showed no remorse about leading the west Atlantic greys towards their end, but how were groups of grey whales faring in other parts of the world? At one time there were four distinct populations of grey whales, one each in the eastern and western Pacific and in the eastern and western Atlantic. Not much is known about the Atlantic populations since both were hunted to extinction before scientists could gather data on their lives. The western Pacific or Korean grey whale still survives – but only just. Once there were up to 10,000 of these magnificent creatures, but their migratory paths along the coast of Asia and the east coast of Japan gave easy access to whalers, who killed them until the population became so depleted that hunting became uneconomic. The Korean greys were virtually wiped out and their numbers haven't recovered even today. Sparse recent sightings may indicate that their fate may be extinction.

Their counterparts on the opposite coast halfway across the globe have never truly been on the brink of extirpation. From the 4000 that remained at the turn of the century, the population began a slow recovery until a new era of slaughter began in 1912 when the Norwegians harpooned their first. The Americans, Japanese and Russians soon followed this lead. As greys were few and far between, the catch rate was low – only about 1000 animals over the next thirty years. Even so, this depleted and endangered species wasn't recognized as such until 1946, when at last it received complete protection. There was one proviso: aboriginal peoples would be allowed to kill whales for subsistence. Russian native peoples who live on the coast of the Chukchi Sea take 179 whales each year, even today. The grey whale was given even more security by the Mexican government in the 1970s, when access to the major calving lagoons was restricted. With these safe havens to give birth, and a migratory route that's virtually harpoon-free, the grey whale has made a remarkable recovery. Today there are probably as many grey whales as at any time in history. Swimming steadily northwards, our mother and calf are just two of a population of over 20,000.

Beyond Vancouver Island the mother and calf swim past the Queen Charlotte Islands, hugging the shoreline as they negotiate the Gulf of Alaska. This far north, nature is at its most pristine. The calf lifts her head out of the grey sea dimpled with raindrops. She can hear the haunting wild calls of loons (divers) carried on the wind. These birds make their eerie cry day and night as the males proclaim their territories on lakes and ponds. Spy-hopping to inspect her surroundings, the calf sees that the coastline is rocky and irregular, incised with deep fjords and cloaked with vast tracts of evergreens. This is virgin forest, watered by moisture carried on warm ocean

Nature at its most pristine. The coastline of the North-west Pacific is cloaked in a forest of evergreens. Just off shore a migrating whale relaxes before continuing its journey.

Grey whales have few natural enemies. This giant vertebra came from an animal that died of old age. Since the cessation of whaling, their population has made a remarkable recovery.

winds which bring more than 3000 millimetres of rain every year. The calf submerges and tucks in behind her mother.

When they come up for air, the whales aren't alone. A volcano of water explodes from the sea beside them, followed by a black head with a steeply sloping forehead. The creature spins to show a creamy white patch on its belly and sides. This is a Dall's porpoise, also known as the 'rooster tail' because as it rises to breathe a cone of water comes off its head. This 2.5-metre cetacean seems hyperactive, performing twists and corkscrews in the pressure wave of the adult grey. After accompanying the whales for a kilometre or so, the porpoise leaves to search for fish.

The calf and her mother wend their way through a scatter of islands and islets. Other than the odd mouthful of shrimp and fish, the cow is still sustained by the fat reserves she stored last year. Still relying on her mother's milk, the calf is nourished indirectly by them as well. But it won't be long before they can both gorge on as much food as they can eat.

On the northern rim of the Pacific, the sun hasn't cracked the leaden skies for a week and for much of the day they swim through a sea shrouded with rolling fog. Glistening grey cliffs rise vertiginously to left and right as the whales travel through the Unimak Pass. Nearly all the world's California grey whales funnel through here every summer to reach the Bering Sea and the icy waters of their feeding grounds beyond. The mother and calf are stragglers: 20,000 other greys are scattered ahead of them, with only a few hundred behind.

These Arctic seas are some of the richest on the planet, and the calf drops through a great school of herring. These are potential prey for a creature which she can hear singing close by. He produces a long warbling note which ends in a soft moan. This is a male bearded seal. He has a long glistening white moustache which curls in a spiral at the tips. Algal blooms cloud the water, so the seal can't be seen by the whale and she can't be seen by him. Beardeds are just one of many species of seal found here; there are white whales, porpoises and sealions as well. All of these marine mammals exploit the explosion of food in the short Arctic summer, sharing out the seasonal harvest by feeding on different kinds of prey.

The grey whales have come here because of the community of tiny animals crowded in the ooze on the sea bed. Tube dwelling amphipods are by far the most numerous, making their homes from mud and mucilage. These shrimp-like creatures are about a centimetre long and feed by using their legs and antennae to rake microscopic food, such as diatoms, from the sand. There may be more than 10,000 individuals per square metre, their densely packed tubes giving a shag-pile carpet effect on the sea floor. Many other creatures live in this miniature forest; some even attach themselves to the amphipods' straw-like houses. Other more mobile types of amphipods have no permanent homes but weave through this dense mat like rocket-propelled cars. Amphipods make up to 90 per cent of the grey whales' diet, which they gather in their own inimitable way.

Clues to how they actually do this can be seen on the calf's mother on the right side of her head. The encrusted barnacles are rubbed away and the baleen on that side is also worn. Another clue comes from the fact that, on the feeding grounds, her head and flanks can be besmeared with mud. In shallow water the calf copies her mother's technique. Gracefully both animals turn on to their right side and then both animals swim forward, skimming over the top layer of sediment. They open their mouths and retract their massive tongues – the adult cow's weighs just over a tonne. Mud is drawn in by the resulting suction and forced through the baleen fringe on the other side of their mouths. Any invertebrate prey is strained out by the comb-like baleen and then scraped off by the tongue. As the whales rise up to the surface, clouds of sand and mud billow from their lips. They extract as much animal food as they can from the mouthful of mud, before taking a breath and ducking down to slurp up another. When mud-skimming, most grey whales turn onto their right sides and that's why the baleen and barnacles on that side become worn.

The mother and calf will continue their great natural journey to the edge of the ice; since reaching the feeding grounds they can feast as they travel. The whales produce a crater each time they suction-feed and thousands of them doing this seems to devastate the sea floor. As our calf swims northwards, she passes over areas where more than 40 per cent of the sea floor is pocked with recently formed feeding pits. This seems as destructive as open-cast mining – but surprisingly grey whales are unwitting market gardeners and actually help to cultivate marine life.

When they churn up the sea floor the grey whales' excavations trap large amounts of organic debris. This debris attracts animal colonists which proliferate in the new territory. The whales feed their crops of amphipods extra food as well; by stirring up the bottom they release nutrients into the water column. This, in turn, stimulates the growth of the plankton on which the amphipods feed.

The market gardening whales encourage amphipods to settle in their feed-

ing craters in another way as well. By grading the particles on the sea floor as they feed, grey whales unwittingly provide the perfect bed for the amphipod crop to thrive in. Every time they spit out a mouthful of sea floor, the heavy sand and grit sinks very quickly while lightweight clay and fine silt are carried by water currents away from the feeding grounds. Without the feeding activities of the whales, the sandy habitats that amphipods prefer could easily be covered by the mud that is discharged by the Yukon and other large Alaskan rivers into the Bering Sea. Grey whales sift 158 million tonnes of sediment every year, an amount nearly three times greater than the sediment discharged annually from the mighty Yukon river.

Whenever the calf and mother vacuum the sea bed, mud flows behind them like the wake of a ship. This is of great benefit to the seabirds which breed on the tundra and sea cliffs. St Lawrence Island in the north of the Bering Sea hosts noisy colonies of kittiwakes and guillemots: every ledge, however precarious, is crammed with jostling birds. As they gouge the sea floor in a shallow bay, our two grey whales are trailed by birds gathering food for their chicks. Just as the calf surfaces and blows, a flock of black-legged kittiwakes arrive at the mud plume

In the ice-strewn waters of the feeding grounds, food is plentiful. The whales feed by sucking in mud and straining out any tiny animals it contains through their comb-like baleens (opposite).

behind her. She's unconcerned by all these flying creatures which dash, hover and dip to seize morsels in their pale yellow beaks.

The rapidly settling sediment just behind the whale's mouth attracts brown birds with a white flash on their bills. Closely watched by the calf, Brunnich's guillemots fly underwater, twisting and curving through the muddy plume. At the surface slightly farther away there is a flotilla of red phalaropes. The adults are breeding on marshy tundra near the coast; those bobbing on the sea are immature birds, white with a pale grey back and a black mark passing through and behind their eyes. They peck daintily in the slick behind the whales. Small creatures and fragments of larger ones are lost through the baleen when greys forage. In this way food that wouldn't otherwise be available is delivered to surface waters to kittiwakes, guillemots and phalaropes. The leftovers from all the greys on the feeding grounds provide food for several hundred thousand seabirds every summer.

Leaving the Bering Sea behind, our calf and her mother enter the Chukchi Sea, the third and most northerly of their odyssey. On some days prevailing winds and currents fill their route with floating ice. The two whales are in the domain of a creature that often drifts on these freezing rafts. Idling in shallow water, the calf comes across her first when she makes out a glimmer of white through the murk. The owner of these metre-long tusks soon cruises into view – weighing about a tonne, the walrus is like an enormous leather bag.

These extraordinary creatures forage on the sea bed, sometimes close to our two whales. Walruses gather prey in areas of muddier or coarser gravel sediment; these are often adjacent to the sandy feeding grounds of the greys. When they forage they push their heads along the bottom and locate hidden prey with their whiskers. Walruses gouge out long sinuous furrows – not pits like the whales. Whenever they find shellfish, the mainstay of their diet, our calf can hear they have been successful: there is an audible slurp as the walrus uses considerable force to suck its meal out of the shell. As there are 200,000 walruses in the Bering and Chukchi Seas, our whale calf will come across them often.

The calf is nearly weaned and rarely suckles now. She and her mother are on the northern boundary of the grey whales' summer territory. Almost all of the other greys here are mothers and calves like themselves; single females and bulls are in the major feeding areas to the south. It seems likely that in the more northerly area, there are fewer killer whales and so the calves are safer.

Lifting her head above the waves, our calf sees a glistening white horizon – a line of solid ice. Her trek is over. She's completed one of the longest journeys made by any mammal. The waters of her distant nursery are 30 degrees centigrade warmer than here on the edge of the pack ice. She's learnt about navigational cues and predators, and now has the skills for a life of travel.

Greys make their annual migrations because their vulnerable babies need to spend the first months of their lives in warm, sheltered waters. But these waters contain few nutrients, and food of the right sort is scarce. To sustain themselves during the breeding season and to eat enough food to grow so huge, greys have no choice but to go to high-latitude seas every summer. Our calf and her mother spend the long Arctic days gorging on amphipods. Over the next few months the cow restores her reserves of blubber to a thickness of 30 centimetres whilst our calf grows and grows.

It's October and the days are getting shorter. When our calf spy-hops she can feel a chill in the air and the surface of what used to be open water begins to congeal with ice. To avoid getting trapped the whales must swim south. Until they reach southern California our calf journeys with the cow, but the bond between them weakens naturally during the southward migration. Now fully independent, the calf leaves her mother to explore on her own. The cow gives no outward sign of registering that her calf has gone. She must continue to San Ignacio lagoon to mate; already she is arousing the interest of bull greys. The calf won't be mature for another two years, and until that time she has no need to journey to the nursery lagoons. For now she explores Monterey Bay, snaffling shrimps that hover in glades in the kelp, spying on sealions performing aquatic pirouettes and bringing exhilaration to whale-watchers who in turn spy upon her. She is a new generation of a magnificent creature that's travelled up and down the Pacific coast for thousands of years.

A western diamondback coils in the shade.
In the Sonoran Desert, the summer sun can
be lethal.

6

THE RATTLESNAKE'S TALE

T HIS HAS BEEN A particularly hard summer even by Sonoran Desert standards — hardly any rain fell during the previous winter. The summer storms, which usually provide some relief to the parched landscape, never delivered their thunderous promise of water. Animals of all kinds have suffered during the drought this year. Many have failed to breed altogether, but some have succeeded. In a deep burrow under a giant saguaro cactus, 2 metres of elegantly scaled, coiled body starts to contract and heave. A large western diamondback rattlesnake (*Crotalus atrox*) is about to give birth.

The rhythmic contractions pulse down her lower half. As her first baby is squeezed from her body she raises her tail, to give it some room. The snakeling, a male, is still wrapped in the glistening birth membranes. These would be on the inside of the shell in egg-laying reptiles but rattlesnakes are ovoviviparous, which means the mother retains the eggs until the young reach full term. Inside her body they are in a relatively safe, moist environment so there is no need for a shell. She even keeps them warm – acting as a mobile incubator by basking in the sun. The new-born baby uses the egg tooth, on the tip of his blunt snout, to slit the birth membranes. Still shining with birth fluid he slides out of the translucent sac. His skin dries and after a few minutes his bright colours and patterns become more obvious. Like other western diamondbacks in this particular region of Arizona his base colour is pinkish brown, and all his tiny black diamond markings are handsomely outlined in white. Perhaps his most striking feature is his tail, which is chalky white and boldly striped with black bands, although there is no rattle yet. His slim body is about 20 centimetres long. His mother suffered during the drought because prey was much harder to come by. Her body's resources have been severely stretched, and forming her eggs was a problem. She simply could not supply some of them with the nourishment they needed. Our male is part of a litter of nine, but two of his siblings are stillborn.

Western diamondbacks have a fearsome reputation. They are usually considered to be dull, dangerous reptiles whose main purpose in life is to bite our livestock and us. In fact they will only waste precious venom on anything too large to eat as a last resort, in self-defence. As for being dull, they have an elegant design and lifestyle for survival under extreme conditions. Their behaviour is often surprisingly sophisticated, and they have an intriguing array of abilities and senses uniquely their own. The biggest surprise is that they navigate to precise destinations on an incredible out-and-back journey.

The seven snakelings are perfect miniature versions of an adult. They are born with fully functional fangs and venom glands. The babies must be able to manage on their own because female rattlesnakes do not pay any attention to their young after they are born. For the first few days the babies won't catch prey as they will be sustained by their large yolk sacs.

The young snakes scatter and disperse from the burrow and find cracks and crevices of their own. Our young male crawls deep inside the decaying skeleton of a dead saguaro cactus. As he slides into his refuge, he flickers his black, deeply forked tongue. This is vital as it helps to give our snake his main sense – that of smell. Although snakes have nostrils and can detect scents in a similar way to most vertebrates, their tongues allow precise detection of chemicals. A rattlesnake uses its tongue to pick up scent. It seems very likely that the two tips give a 'stereo' sense of smell, important for following the scent trails of prey and mates. The two tips enable the rattlesnake to keep on target, because it can tell whether the strongest smell is coming from the left or from the right. Scent molecules from the air and ground are flicked by its tongue tips into its mouth where some reach the ultra-sensitive receptors, known as Jacobsen's organs, in the roof of its mouth. These organs analyse the chemical composition of the molecules and relay the message to the snake's brain.

This supersense will play a key role throughout our snake's life, particularly when he starts to travel. His regular journeys will begin when he is an adult – if he survives that long, as baby rattlesnakes are fair game for most desert predators.

With a gentle descending cry a streamlined shape trots out from behind a creosote bush on powerful legs which end in strong clawed feet, each with two toes pointing forwards and two back. With a flick of its wings it springs up on to a large rock to survey the scene below. This pheasant-sized, jogging bird is a roadrunner – a relative of the cuckoo. He cocks his head to stare down at a patch of cactus below, flicks his tail and elegantly glides down the slope over the dried-up stems of brittlebush and bursage. Landing with a flourish amongst some cholla cactus, he cocks his head again and raises his crest. With a couple of bounding steps the roadrunner starts to investigate the cholla patch for food. These birds are carnivorous, feeding primarily on large insects and small reptiles, although they will eat cactus fruit.

Late summer is a good time for small reptiles, especially young snakes. Our male rattler is secure in a patch of hedgehog cactus, and all he sees of the roadrunner is a blur as it trots past, but another baby rattlesnake is caught out in the open.

The young female reacts to the vibrations of the approaching bird by instinctively rearing up into the famous defence posture of rattlesnakes. Using her lower coils as a steady platform she raises the front half of her body and leans forwards in an aggressive 'S'-shaped stance. As the roadrunner gets dangerously close, she turns to face the threat. She rises up and vibrates the tip of her tail.

Although she tries her best to make a warning noise, she can't. Baby rattlesnakes have only a button at the tip of their tails – the first link of their rattles only appears after their first skin is shed.

The roadrunner knows he must take care with the small venomous diamondback. Using his great agility and skill, he dances round the striking snake and with a quick parry dispatches her with a few well-aimed blows of his powerful beak. After smashing his writhing victim against a small rock, the roadrunner throws his head up and swallows the limp body in one gulp. Fluffing out his feathers, he flicks his tail and trots confidently away in search of more prey.

Because the summer has been so hard there is little food available. The desert is also home to multi-legged and poison-fanged predators and as night falls other creatures that catch rattlesnake babies emerge from their lairs. Our young male is in his cactus refuge, unaware of the potential hazard which scuttles past him like an express train in the middle of the night. This sleek, fast creature with its innumerable long running legs and powerful venom-tipped jaws is *Scolopendra* – a giant centipede. Twenty centimetres long and armour-plated, it is a rapacious predator of all small animals, stalking its victims like a tiny leopard before pouncing and then injecting them with poison. Hand-sized tarantulas are more sedate as they scour the desert for insects, baby rodents and the odd baby snake, retreating by day into silken tunnels.

In a week our male is the only survivor of the litter. The other snakelings have been eaten. The roadrunner had two, a couple more went to tarantulas and the last two were dispatched by giant centipedes.

Our male has now found a deep crevice under a large rock in which to hide. He is about to slough, or shed, his skin. For the last few days his normally bright eyes have been clouded over with a milky fluid and he has been partially blind. Now they have cleared and he begins to push his snout against the walls of his crevice. As he rubs against the rock, he loosens the old skin around the edges of his upper and lower lips and this begins to peel backwards, turning inside out, as it proceeds. The milky fluid helped to loosen the old covering from the new, and after an hour or so of writhing and rubbing the snake is free of his old skin, leaving behind a papery ghost of his former self. The shed skin once covered every part of his body, including his eyes, and the transparent scales which protected his eyeballs now stare out blankly from the empty shroud. When young, he will shed his skin up to six times in a year; this rate will halve in adults. Snakes slough to provide for both growth and wear. Now, at the tip of his tail, our snake has the first segment of the rattle that gives him his name, and he'll add another every time he sheds until by the time he is adult he could have a rattle twelve segments long. Theoretically, the rattle should be longer than this but the outer segments are repeatedly lost through natural wear and tear.

Even though western diamondbacks are fully equipped with venom and fangs at birth, the babies are prey for a multitude of desert hunters from tarantulas and giant centipedes to roadrunners.

Aafter their first slough baby snakes begin to feed. At first young western diamondbacks prey mainly on lizards and very small rodents, and our snake has three whiptail lizards before autumn. In early October, the desert is slightly greener than its baked summer state because a few late storms have delivered some of the rain that the parched earth so desperately needed. Overhead, flocks of migrant birds stream southwards – raptors such as broad-tailed and Swainson's hawks, black and turkey vultures and long chains and 'V'-shaped formations of wildfowl. All are heading south to winter in Mexico and Central or South America as cold weather sweeps down the North American continent, blanketing the far north in ice and snow and bringing frosts and cold squalls to the south.

Extreme cold is lethal to rattlesnakes – if they are caught out in the open, they may freeze. Even if they are not killed directly by the cold, their lethargy or inability to react quickly at low temperatures makes them very vulnerable to attack by predators. Inbuilt instincts warn our snake that he must find a deep, dry shelter that will protect him during the cold months.

Our snake finds a perfect place for hibernation, the old burrow of a kangaroo rat, sheltered under a weeping chain-fruit cholla. The adult rattlesnakes congregate in specific places elsewhere. Our snake won't join them until he is older, when he will start the cycle of travel which will dominate his adult life. For now, however, he hibernates alone.

By the end of his third year our snake is a handsome animal nearly a metre long. It's autumn once more but this year our snake will spend the winter in a place to which he will return every year for the rest of his life. The middle parts of the days are still warm, so when the weather permits he warms up by basking. As he lies on a rock a large male rattlesnake slithers by.

Within a few seconds the other snake has disappeared, leaving a faint trace of scent behind him. Our snake uses his tongue to pick up the trail. Within a couple of hours he leaves the cholla patch where he has spent most of his life so far. Venturing farther afield than ever before, he follows the scent trail in the direction of a craggy bluff which dominates the horizon.

Before long he finds the place where the other snake was heading. Amongst the rocks, on ledges and in open pockets of earth, dozens of rattlesnakes are basking in the late afternoon light.

As the last rays of sun wash over the bluff the snakes disappear into crevices to escape the cold. Our snake is one of the last to enter. As he descends he finds the crack opening out into a small dry chamber. Using his tongue he discovers the scent trails of other adults. This particular south-facing slope contains, in its uneven surface, dozens of small caves and chambers, the best of which are sheltered from the wind and rain and are cool and dry. These are the traditional winter dens or hibernacula where all the adult diamondbacks from the surrounding area come to spend the winter. But the cool, dark chambers attract others too.

A sudden final shaft of light from the setting sun penetrates the tunnel, illuminating the interior with a bright golden glow. The diamondback edges in slightly farther and is slowly sliding over a lip of rock when a monstrous head rears up before him. Its fierce-looking gape and heavy-set jaw give it a menacing, almost prehistoric, look. The lizard's beaded skin is alarmingly patterned with swirling designs of red and black – a warning signal to all who come near it.

This is a Gila monster, one of only two species of venomous lizard in the world (the other is the Mexican beaded lizard). This stocky reptile, some 60 centimetres long, flicks out its notched tongue. Sensing that the new arrival is just another rattlesnake coming to spend the winter, the Gila monster slouches back onto the rocky floor. The lizard is no threat to our snake as it feeds on small mammals, birds and their eggs. It has come to hibernate too and will peacefully share the den with three others of its kind as well as the rattlers.

Here in the Sonoran Desert in Arizona, our snake shares a den with about fifteen others, but some hibernacula hold far more. In the freezing conditions far to the north, fully protective refuges are more necessary. Prairie rattlesnakes gather in huge numbers with up to 1000 assembling in a favoured hibernaculum. However, winter is not so harsh in Arizona, so specifications for a den – like depth – are not so stringent. As there are many more sites that are adequate, western diamondbacks don't have to gather in dense concentrations.

The desert does not shut down completely in the winter. As the blustery seasonal squalls of rain buffet the bluff and rock the tall saguaros, the desert begins to change colour. It gradually turns to various shades of green as the cacti and other plants take advantage of the moisture. While our snake is snug inside the slope, the earth across this whole region receives its first good soaking for nearly two years.

A magical process is starting in the soil. As the water penetrates deeper it triggers huge numbers of tiny seeds, whose inbuilt chemical factories now start to burn the fuel they have stored for so long. Thousands of seed-coats crack as the embryo plants swell, and tiny roots hatch out to make tentative forays into the earth. Although it's still too cold for them to start growing properly, the repeated bouts of rain and even the odd snow shower have started a chain reaction in the soil, which holds promise for a spectacular spring.

This begins in late February when it's warm enough for the snakes to emerge from the hibernaculum in the middle of each day to bask in the sun. Little flurries of high, wispy cloud are the only features in the largely clear blue sky. Warmth and moisture are the required formula and, all around, thousands of seedlings are springing up, carpeting the open areas with green.

Early one afternoon, our snake is sunbathing when crescent-shaped shadows race over his body. Exuberant, musical screams shatter the calm of the early afternoon up on the bluff, and arcing shapes chase each other as they twist and turn through the sky. A gang of aeronautes is playing tag. Aeronautes, or white-throated swifts, fully deserve their Latin name for they fly through the sky

Adult western diamondbacks hibernate communally in dry, secure chambers on rocky slopes of bluffs. Up to two dozen diamondbacks may overwinter in these hibernacula which may have been used for generations.

to snap up small insects like missiles with wings. At this time of year there is an additional purpose to their reckless aerobatics – sexual politics.

White-throated swifts are such brilliant fliers that they can actually mate in mid-air. The males catch the females high in the sky and the coupled pair spiral down together, separating just before they reach the ground. Some of the groups of swifts darting around the bluff are trios and look as if they are playing follow-my-leader. The threesomes twist and turn as if they have all learned the moves of a complex aerial ballet. In fact these groups probably consist of two male swifts and a female. The female is the leader of the group and she is closely followed by her mate, while the third is an interloper. This third swift has already mated with his chosen partner, but is trying to steal an extra coupling on the side. The second swift closely trails his mate, making every effort to ensure that no other male, no matter how skilled an aerobat, gets the chance to mate with his female. As a trio skims past, out beyond the bluff, our basking snake's reproductive instincts are awakening too. For the first time he's old enough to breed.

All over the sunny slope small groups of snakes lie out a few metres from the entrances to their hibernacula. This proximity makes it easy for males to

In the Sonoran Desert the bizarre Gila (pronounced 'heela') monster sometimes hibernates with western diamondbacks in the same dens. It is one of only two species of venomous lizard in the world.

locate females – many of them mate right outside the winter dens. Each female advertises her willingness by exuding a cocktail of chemical messengers, or pheromones, from her skin. A gentle breeze wafts a strong sexual scent towards our male, enticing him further down the slope where he finds a young female draped over a low shelf of rock. Flicking his tongue rapidly, the male instinctively initiates the preliminaries to mating. He repeatedly nudges her with his head, and starts to caress her long body with his chin.

Suddenly a shadow crosses the male's face, distracting him from his foreplay. He turns from his potential mate and stares straight into the unblinking gaze of another, larger, male diamondback. Unlike some mammals and birds, this staring out isn't an aggressive signal. All snakes lack eyelids, so they can never close their eyes: awake or asleep, the serpent eye remains fixed in a glassy stare.

The newcomer is intent on mating with the female himself. He slams his body into our snake and the pair begin a duel. They entwine and raise up the front part of their bodies. They sway in a sinuous dance, sometimes with their heads a full 50 centimetres above the ground. This ritualized combat is so balletic and graceful that it was once thought to be the pre-nuptial display of a pair, but it always involves two males. Each of the combatants attempts to push the other's head to the ground. This jousting is ritual and the snakes don't risk injury by bringing their fangs into play. In this instance the bout continues for forty minutes before the larger animal pins down our snake. Exhausted, our rattlesnake crawls away.

In combat dances the victor is nearly always the larger snake who has superior strength and endurance. However, the successful male doesn't always get to mate. During the bout, the female slithered away and is mating with another male higher up the slope.

The following morning dawns as a perfect spring day. The air is thick with the sound of humming insects and singing birds. It's time for our diamond-back to leave his winter home; he does not return to the cholla patch where he grew up, but instead sets a course to the west – out into the plain. He's embarking on the first great summer journey of his life.

Before he sets off our snake warms himself in the April sun. Like other reptiles he is cold-blooded. The term is actually misleading, since reptiles often have a blood temperature warmer than that of humans. The difference is that they rely on external sources of heat to bring their metabolism up to its operating temperature, which for rattlesnakes is 27-32 degrees centigrade. Mammals and birds, in contrast, generate heat internally through metabolic processes: to fuel this internal central heating they have to eat regularly. Since snakes don't expend any energy keeping their body temperature up, they can survive for months without food.

Basking for brief periods in direct sun, or hugging a warm rock, are two ways in which reptiles can raise their body temperature. But as the sun climbs higher the air itself heats up, enabling them to get their bodies up to speed without the need to sunbathe. It's a surprising fact that too much sun can kill rattlesnakes very quickly. Today temperatures reach 45 degrees centigrade in the direct sun and, elegantly coiled, our snakes rests in a shady brittlebush thicket. If he was trapped out in the open in the direct sun he would very quickly overheat: after only a few minutes his muscles would suffer irreparable damage, and after ten to twelve minutes he would be baked alive.

When the diamondback leaves the slope, he enters a world dominated by cacti. He skirts a colony of low cholla cacti, just like the ones amongst which he spent his early years. The cacti are dotted all around amongst the rocks and sandy, ochre earth; unlike the snakes they can't slide away into the shade when the sun gets too hot. They have to rely on other tricks to protect themselves from the burning heat. Each plant has stubby branches consisting of what look like chains of green potatoes – actually cactus pads – covered in spiky blond hair. This is really a thick carpet of long spines, and some chollas are so densely covered in these spines that they look furry; because of this, one of the species is called teddy bear cholla. The pale colour and reflective surface of the spines form a sun-screen for the cactus, preventing the delicate surface of the pads from being cooked. The dense thicket of spines may also help reduce water loss by acting as a windbreak, trapping a layer of humid air amongst the spines to cloak the whole cactus in a moist envelope.

Chollas are close relations of the prickly pear, and they grow in a similar way. However, cholla pads, unlike those of prickly pear, are actually designed to drop off. The outermost pads are only weakly joined to the mother branch and can be knocked off with the slightest touch. The hooked spines not only defend the plant from the unwanted attention of peccaries, deer and cattle but their barbed tips are perfect for hooking into hide, skin and fur for hitching a free ride. Before long the irritated animal will scratch or knock the cactus pad from its body. If a pad falls onto suitable ground it will slowly take root and form a new cholla plant.

After passing through the cholla patch the snake

OVERLEAF: In March, western diamondbacks start a journey to find or return to summer feeding grounds. To begin with it is cool enough to be out during the day but as summer progresses they will only journey at night.

glides over richer, softer soil, where the rain has created large fans of red earth over the flat land. Towards evening the weather is pleasantly warm, and he moves through a forest of saguaros, the largest cacti in the Sonoran Desert.

Ten metres up on the towering tip of a stately saguaro branch a pair of white-winged doves perch amongst a ring of swelling flower buds which garland the end of each of the cactus's spiny arms. These buds will open into large waxy flowers in May, when most of the other spring flowers are over. These flowers are at their most glorious now and the birds look down at our snake as he winds through a kaleidoscope of reds, yellows, oranges and blues. As far as the doves can see, the desert is a riot of spring flowers – the legacy of generous winter rains. All those seeds that were brought to life as the water saturated the earth in the preceding months have now reached their climax.

The doves soon lose sight of the rattlesnake as he sinks further into a sea of brilliant orange – desert poppies, whose satin petals glint and flare as they face the sun. Slightly farther away a lone, portly barrel cactus stands guard over a sea of rich blue lupins, its own vermilion flowers standing out in brilliant contrast. Beyond the barrel cactus flutter great drifts of desert gold, their delicate flowers dancing gracefully on the wind.

Our snake is sliding along at a good pace for a rattlesnake; his body forms an elegant series of 'S'-shaped curves which ripple down from head to tail in a continuous motion as alternate blocks of muscle along his spine relax and contract. This motion gives our snake a line of pivoting points along his body, to push against irregularities in the ground to propel him forward. This lateral undulation is the most common method of snake movement but heavy-bodied species, such as rattlesnakes, pythons and vipers, can also move in another way by a method called rectilinear creeping. Instead of throwing their bodies into curves, they gently ripple their stomach muscles to push groups of belly scales against the ground, while sliding others forwards; this gives the general impression that they are gliding slowly along in a straight line.

A week later the snake is nearly 2 kilometres away from the foot of the bluff, and far away from the place of his birth. In the late morning, as the sun starts to feel a little too warm, he hides in the shade of a magnificent saguaro with five huge arms. The saguaro is growing on a low crest of land whose southern slope is dotted with patches of open earth and sprawling paloverde trees.

Mature saguaros can be over 200 years old. They grow very slowly. Saguaros, throughout their long lives, become increasingly top-heavy as the great arms – each one can weigh over a tonne – increase in girth. This can lead to the death of really big individuals, as they can be blown over during severe storms.

Our snake is just moving down off the edge of the crest, away from the saguaro and amongst the paloverdes, when the ground around him bursts into strange vibrations. The snake tenses, all his senses alerted. The vibrations come in pulses and are accompanied by rapid ripples of tiny movements which fuse together so that the earth seems to buzz beneath him. Suddenly there is a scuffle in the ground a few centimetres in front of him, and the snake snatches back his head as a large, black, armoured abdomen hauls itself out of the earth.

After another scuffle the head and shoulders of a vast female wasp emerge from the tunnel. In her jaws she has a huge, hairy tarantula. The wasp, a tarantula hawk, is a striking insect, shiny black with two sturdy pairs of iridescent reddish wings. She almost brushes over our snake as she hauls the still form of the giant spider away across the sand.

The large wasp has fought and stung the tarantula to immobilize it. She is taking the live but paralysed arachnid to another chamber that she excavated earlier. Once there, she will haul her load inside and – after leaving an egg on the spider's body – she'll seal the entrance. After a few days the egg will hatch and her grub will have fresh tarantula meat to feast on. After demolishing the spider, the grub will pupate, becoming part of next spring's generation of tarantula hawks.

At the beginning of May, the temperatures keep on rising. The snake continues his journey, travelling whenever he chooses. He's now a little over 3 kilometres from the slope of the bluff. Western diamondbacks don't travel in long, dedicated bursts like many other animal travellers; instead they wander slowly, often stopping for days to investigate certain areas. This is particularly true of our snake on this, his first summer journey. He is looking for a rich feeding area to which he may return for many years to come. But, he's not a fast mover and can't cover large distances. He must also hunt en route and this slows him down further – he has to stop regularly and hide, to lie in wait for prey.

Most small rodents only come out after dark, which makes them tricky targets for predators which rely on vision to find their prey. But rattlesnakes are well equipped for hunting in low light and even darkness, as they have other means of locating their victims. For them, catching a mouse is largely a matter of being in

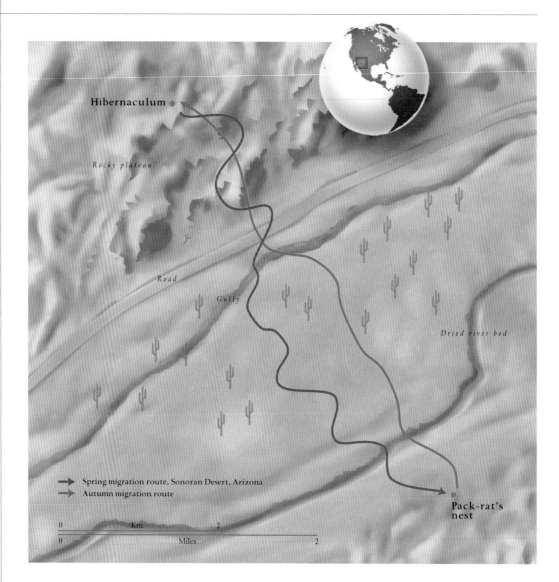

Hibernaculum

Rocky plateau

Road

Gully

Dried river bed

Spring migration route, Sonoran Desert, Arizona
Autumn migration route

Pack-rat's
nest

0   Km   2
0   Miles   2

the right place at the right time. Our snake moves out from under a fallen saguaro limb and finds a gap between two large boulders. He tests the ground with his tongue and senses a faint trace of prey. As the evening sky starts to glow, he takes up position and waits.

From under the drooping branches of a chain-fruit cholla, a small, furtive shape hops, stops and then jumps amongst the uneven, prickled skirt of linked cactus fruit. She repeatedly stops to sniff the air. Her twitching nose cannot find anything on the breeze to cause alarm and she can hear no movement around her.

Relaxing a little, she starts to clean herself in the dark moon shadows of the cactus. She's 18 centimetres long from her nose to the brush at the tip of her long whip-like tail. With a warm sandy brown pelt and a pair of very long, muscular hind legs, she seems strangely proportioned for such a small rodent. But these legs are her main form of defence and she gets her name from them: she's a kangaroo rat. These powerful hindquarters give her the ability to clear 60 centimetres in a single jump, in any direction. Like others of her kind she's extremely well equipped for life in the desert. She possesses a pair of some of the most efficient kidneys in the mammalian world – she's a specialist in water conservation.

Tonight she's out looking for the dry seeds which form the bulk of her diet. Although such seeds are full of energy-giving carbohydrate, they have a water content of only 4 per cent but this is sufficient. Her metabolism can extract all the moisture she needs from such dry foods. Unlike most mammals, which must flush out their uric waste with copious amounts of water, this creature can concentrate her urine until it is almost a paste. She rarely urinates, but when she does its thick consistency means that hardly any of her body's water is wasted.

She hops out beyond the protective cover of the cactus and tests the air again for any sign of danger. With a couple of hops she crosses the little clearing in front of the cactus which shelters her burrow and reaches a little gap between two large boulders. Ever cautious, she sniffs the air once more and enters the gap.

Our snake is immediately alerted to her presence by the tiny vibrations that her feet make on the ground, and now he forms a thermal image of the rat. Western diamondbacks, like all rattlesnakes, belong to a family of snakes called pit vipers. They have two deep pits at the front of their heads just under the smaller and less obvious nostrils. These pits are heat-seeking organs, giving these snakes the ability to form a thermal image of their prey – allowing them to see in pitch-darkness. At close range a warm-blooded animal's body stands out against its colder background, allowing the snake to take aim accurately.

As the kangaroo rat stops to nibble on a couple of seeding grassheads, a shape explodes from a crevice and slams into her left thigh, jabbing two tiny points deep into her flesh. The impact smashes her into the hard wall of the boulder. With a panicked squeal, she bunches her huge thigh muscles and powers vertically up and away. Pivoting elegantly in mid-air, she clears the boulder and lands back in the clearing with a racing heart and pounding lungs. There is no escape, however; as she rushes back to her burrow her situation worsens. As she moves, her beating heart pumps the lethal venom throughout her body.

During the strike our snake's hollow fangs, which normally lie folded back along the roof of his mouth, swivelled forwards into their attack position. As they made contact with the kangaroo rat, muscles squeezed glands behind each of our snake's eyes. A high pressure jet of venom was then injected into the victim through a duct in the fangs. Rattlesnake venom contains some components that cause the prey's nervous system to malfunction and others that attack muscles and blood vessels. This lethal cocktail is designed to debilitate and kill prey quickly, and then to break down the body tissues, kick-starting the process of digestion – an important characteristic when meals are so large. Hijacking a creature with chemicals is one of the greatest of snake accomplishments. This technique allows minimal physical contact with any potentially dangerous prey.

Back in her burrow, the kangaroo rat's body systems are beginning to malfunction: her breathing becomes shallower and her legs won't work properly. She tries to stand but falls over repeatedly. Over the next few minutes her movements lessen until finally she loses consciousness.

The rattlesnake emerges from under the boulder, his flicking 'V'-shaped tongue tests the air. As he scouts round the edge of the clearing, the moonlight picks out his intricately patterned body, revealing the lines of dark, linked diamond marks along his backbone. He soon finds a trace of his victim's scent and tracks its jinking path. The snake is in no hurry – his paralysed prey won't be going anywhere. He tongue-flicks repeatedly as he finds his way to the kangaroo rat's body.

A snake's inwardly curved teeth are useless for chewing but these reptiles have the ability to swallow an item of food which, in size, exceeds the diameter of their own heads. To achieve this feat, our snake seeks out the front of the kangaroo rat. Swallowing prey head-first ensures that the limbs will fold easily rather than being bent back the wrong way and possibly snagging on the sides of the snake's throat. When he's sure he's at the right end, our snake opens his jaws and the rat is dragged into his gullet by his teeth which are alternately freed and re-fastened in a ratchet-type mechanism. The neck muscles are then brought into play, forcing the meal towards the stomach. The going is easy until the shoulders, the widest part of the rat's body. Our rattlesnake takes a long time to get past these, and to avoid choking he thrusts his reinforced windpipe out of the side of his mouth to breathe. It seems as if he has unhinged his jaws, but no snakes do this. The bones in their jaws are joined by muscles and ligaments which give the enormous flexibility and elasticity needed for a huge gape. As the bulk of the rat's body passes down our snake's gullet, his outer covering is stretched so that the scales are pulled apart, but his skin is so flexible it will not tear. He lifts up his head as the tassel on the tip of the rat's tail finally disappears into his mouth. Our rattlesnake re-aligns his jaws with a few grimace-like stretches. For a few days, as he lies up to digest his meal, his journey will be stalled.

Spring wanes and the heat of summer takes over. All around, the ground is drying out and the plants are turning brown. The cacti are peppered with developing fruit, and the once-colourful tapestry of annuals has disappeared as one by one the flowers died. However, during their short life, most were pollinated and millions of tiny seeds lie dormant. Each must now wait for a future winter with good rain before they too emerge and create another spectacular cycle of exuberant reproduction.

By late May it's getting too hot to be out in the daytime and the diamondback has to hide during the day, only travelling during the cool of the night. By now our snake is well out on to the plain. A grand old saguaro stands on its crest of land, dominating this part of the desert. From its highest point a large dark shape opens its soft wings and floats silently away across the land. The great horned owl is the largest owl in North America and ranges from high up near the Arctic tundra right down into Mexico. This adaptable bird is found in a huge variety of habitats, and has no problem surviving here in the desert.

Our snake is hidden away under an agave plant when, on whispering wings, the owl swoops past to land on top of a large barrel cactus. After shaking his feathers the owl calls loudly to his mate, who responds with an equally sonorous cry. The snake, however, hears nothing, as all snakes are stone-deaf. They don't have external ears or eardrums and therefore cannot hear airborne vibrations in the same way that humans can. Instead, some bones in their head are modified to be incredibly sensitive to vibrations in the ground. So our snake continues on his journey, oblivious of the owls' nocturnal duet.

A few days and a couple of hundred metres later, the diamondback encounters a surface he's never experienced before. Unlike the ever-changing textures of the desert, this is very uniform and compacted. Although he's nervous about such a large open area, he slithers onto it. Halfway across he detects the smell of decay. Turning to his left he investigates the remains of a small mammal. However he doesn't feed on carrion, so after a couple of flicks of his tongue he moves on. He has less than a metre to go when his whole world starts to shake.

This rattlesnake is striking at 3 metres per second, although they have a top speed of 4. This seems fast but it's actually slower than a man striking with his fist.

Snakes never dislocate their jaws when feeding. The bones in their skulls are joined by muscles and ligaments, this flexibility and elasticity are enough to allow them a gape huge enough to swallow prey.

Within seconds the terrifying vibrations reach fever pitch and our snake coils in alarm as a colossal dark shape bears down on him. The rumbling, rushing, living earthquake goes past with incredible speed, its spinning edge passing within centimetres of his delicate rattle. Immediately afterwards the snake is swamped in a bitter, sulphurous cloud of fumes, and his back is stung by flying debris and a howling, dusty wind. When the vibrations of the truck are over he uncoils and glides over the sand at the edge of the road, and finds his way to a steep gully leading to a dry river bed.

As dawn tints the desert a soft pink, a female mule deer delicately picks her way along the river bed, stopping every now and then to nibble on some of the greener vegetation along the banks. After a few minutes the doe scans the desert and decides to leave the river bed; she soon spots a gully and starts to climb.

Warned by strong vibrations as the large mammal approaches, the diamondback reacts quickly. He coils the back part of his body into a widely opened loop. Above this he raises the front part of his body with his head and neck in a large 'S'-shaped wave. Hissing loudly and rattling furiously, he presents an alarming spectacle. This is no empty threat; as a last resort he only needs to straighten the wave in his neck to release a dangerous strike. The doe snorts in alarm and backs off. Although nervous of the sound, she is also curious and doesn't go far.

The deer is close enough for our snake's heat sensors to pick her up — these confirm that nearby there is a large and potentially dangerous creature. To emphasize his warning he rises still further from his coils. His head and neck are like a poised and threatening lance which tracks the deer as she moves to the left and then to the right.

His rattle, a key part of this display, consists of interlinked segments. The noise is created by each of the hollow segments rattling against the surface of its neighbour, not by objects rattling around inside like a child's rattle. Each segment has an intricate articulation point which gives several points of contact. As the snake rapidly vibrates the string these points of contact generate sound, which is amplified further by the hollow interior of each individual segment. Although the diamondback can't hear the noise himself, it certainly affects the deer in front of him. At last the doe decides that she has seen and heard enough, and retreats.

Rattlesnakes evolved their threatening display just for this purpose, as a warning to keep away. Unless their lives are at risk from being trodden on, for instance, they are not aggressive to animals larger than themselves. Their venom is precious — it takes a lot of energy to produce, and they need this resource for dispatching their prey. A bite in self-defence is always a last resort.

A couple of days after his encounter with the truck and the deer, the snake continues his travels. He crosses a dry river with its covering of bleached pebbles and finds himself in a rocky patch of cacti and scrub, rich with the scent of rodents. He's now nearly 5 kilometres from the bluff with the hibernaculum.

On a warm evening in late June, when our snake is exploring, he picks up an interesting smell with his tongue. A trail leads along a ridge of rocks to an untidy mound of cactus litter. The mound is over a metre in both diameter and height and lying on its top are some ring pulls from cans of soft drink. The creature that dwells in the mound is attracted to the shiny objects to such a degree that, to pick them up, it will drop other nest material it is carrying. It is this behaviour which gave the trade or pack-rat its name.

Our rattlesnake slithers inside the mound. The occupant, an adult rat, nibbles on a cactus fruit and is taken by surprise – the snake strikes at the rodent before it has a chance to flee. After eating the owner, our rattlesnake takes up residence in the mound.

Over the next few weeks he uses this new refuge as a permanent base from which to explore the area. This is a rich hunting ground with a high density of pack-rats and other small mammals. For the next few months this is journey's end. He builds up a detailed mental map of his new domain. In the future, unless the habitat changes or the supply of rodents dries up he will navigate back to this precise spot, probably even residing in the exact same pack-rat mound, year after year.

One August night our snake is foraging. Thunderous storms move in from the south, pounding the sandy ground with torrential rain. Puffs of dust fly as the first huge drops slam into the ground around our snake. At this time of year he is at no risk from cold, so he stays out in the storm.

Deep in the soil other bodies are stirring. Spade-foot toads lie dormant in the ground for months, or even years, waiting for good summer storms to flood parts of the desert. If sufficient moisture falls and soaks the earth, the toads will emerge from their long sleep and, like many of the desert plants, embark on their own very rapid reproductive cycle.

Great spikes of lightning shatter the sky, catching the diamondback by the side of a large pool. Already the water is swarming with dozens of spade-foots, the males calling wildly as each tries to grasp a slippery mate. The small amphibians

Evening in high summer: the shadows lengthen and the saguaro cacti are dyed orange by the setting sun. As the heat of the day begins to dissipate, rattlesnakes will begin their wanderings.

The rattlesnake's territory is dwindling as much of the Sonoran Desert disappears beneath concrete and dwellings. Snakes of many species can become casualties when crossing roads.

don't have much time – a matter of weeks at the most. After spawning, their tadpoles must reach maturity before the ponds dry up.

Adult rattlesnakes feed almost exclusively on mammalian prey, so our snake ignores the toads. He can survive for months without drinking, but he will if there's an opportunity to do so. His tongue flickers to test the water, but it plays no part in drinking. He submerges much of his head so that both mouth and nostrils are below the surface. As he draws in water, the sides of his head ripple with rhythmic movements. With each draught he slightly opens his mouth.

The long summer draws on; cooler temperatures now enable our snake to remain active in the daytime once more. After nearly eight fruitful weeks in the pack-rat den, he's extremely well fed. His instincts urge him to start wandering again. Around him the desert is greener, and all over the plain other rattlesnake travellers have left their summer dens. Western diamondbacks have an autumn breeding season as well as a spring one and the rain has acted as a stimulus, encouraging them to search for mates.

Our diamondback heads slowly back over the ground he covered weeks before. He's in no particular rush and explores the drying river which is dotted with pools – remnants of brief storm floods – and safely winds his way back over the road. He soon climbs over the crest of rocks where the pupa of a tarantula hawk is waiting for spring. One balmy day in early autumn he basks under the arms of an old saguaro when a distinctive scent suddenly distracts him.

Uncoiling rapidly, he glides round the old cactus's sturdy base. It has lost one of its mighty arms during the violent thunderstorms and now a long shape moves gracefully over this spiny green wall. The female rattlesnake notices our male and stops.

She wasn't mated in the spring and, like our male, has had a good summer. The male gently approaches and tentatively nudges her sleek and well fed body with his head, testing her scales with a frenzy of tongue flicking. Chemical messengers, or pheromones, exuding from her skin confirm she is in breeding condition. He caresses her jerkily, rubbing his chin all along her body. This time he isn't disturbed by a larger male and when she is responsive he moves his tail under hers and his erect twin-headed hemipenis. This handy organ enables a male snake to copulate with a female from whichever side of his body is convenient. Either one of the double lobes can be used, depending on which one is facing the appropriate direction at the appropriate time.

A fortnight after he mated, our snake feels a distinct chill in the evening air. This is a signal for him to return to the hibernaculum, as before too long winter will arrive. Leaving the old saguaro behind he sets off, picking up clues from the ground and air with his forked tongue. Guided by his inbuilt tracking ability he heads in the direction of the craggy bluff.

All across the desert diamondbacks are doing the same, and by the time our snake is crossing the bare washes of earth which, in spring, had been a carpet of poppies he starts to meet up with more and more of his own kind. As the nights are cool the snakes are often out in the daytime at this time of year. As they converge on the lower slopes of the bluff, their concentrated numbers attract unwelcome attention. Some of the rattlesnakes fall prey to red-tailed hawks, but there is danger at ground level too.

The late afternoon sun strikes a sinuous form as 1.5 metres of black and white banded reptile skims over the stony ground amongst the dried grass stems. This is a female king snake, a strong, active predator of a wide variety of desert life. She is excited by the numerous scent trails that she crosses as she races amongst the rocks. She locks on to a target and approaches a basking rattlesnake. She lunges in a moment, clamping onto our diamondback with her recurved teeth and throwing a couple of muscular coils round his delicately patterned body. King snakes are not venomous but subdue their prey by constriction. During this process their coils draw inexorably tighter until their prey loses consciousness because it is unable to breathe.

Desperate to shake the king snake off, our rattlesnake bites her neck. It's very hard for him to get a grip on her writhing body and his fangs glance off her scales, only managing to inject a small amount of venom. The king snake continues her attempts to subdue him — what little venom she received has no effect because king snakes have some immunity to rattlesnake toxins. The two snakes flail and writhe as one tries to escape and the other struggles for a better grip. Finally, when both are exhausted, the king snake loosens her coils. She miscalculated: our diamondback is just too large. He's nearly the same size as her and even if she had overpowered him she would have found him difficult to swallow. Suddenly she releases her grip and glides away in search of easier prey.

That evening our snake reaches the flat rocks just outside the hibernaculum. He can probably locate the den sites with his heat-sensing organs, as the rocks retain their warmth and stand out against the colder background of the air and vegetation. He pauses at the cave entrance to test the air. Behind him, out in the desert, the old saguaro where he mated is silhouetted against the setting sun. Beyond the cactus a lone pair of car headlights shine. The white beam speeding across the land acts as a reminder that the desert territory of rattlesnakes is

dwindling rapidly. These newcomers and their machines could threaten all Sonoran desert life. To the side of the road, not far from the river bed, a pack-rat washes in the safety of a large deserted mound it found two weeks ago, nestled between a ridge of low rocks and an old mesquite tree. The mound won't always be safe for the rodent. If our diamondback survives hibernation he will return there next summer.

Our diamondback has completed his first round trip. If the habitat remains unchanged he'll travel this same route in the coming years. His journey is only a few kilometres, but for a supposedly dull reptile, which until recently was thought to wander aimlessly, it's still an impressive feat. To navigate from his winter quarters to a precise destination on the summer feeding grounds he uses his amazing geographical memory, sense of smell, heat-sensing ability and, perhaps, other senses as yet undiscovered.

For now he will hibernate but in the spring, when he and the other diamondbacks begin to journey once again, right across the globe other animal travellers will also be on the move. Far to the north, in Labrador, the caribou herds will feel a familiar restlessness. It won't be long before the cows must trek to their calving grounds on the tundra. In Mexico, to the south, the strengthening sun will stimulate millions of monarch butterflies to invade the United States once more. West of these great insect colonies, grey whales will be giving birth to calves. Soon young and old will swim virtually the whole length of the Pacific coast of North America to their summer destination in the freezing Arctic seas. Above another continent, barn swallows that wintered in South Africa will begin their marathon flight to Europe. Even farther to the east beneath the sea off the coast of Australia, a marathon swim will be under way. Mature short-finned eels will travel back to where they were spawned. All of these journeys are perilous, and there will be many casualties along the way, but some of the travellers have always reached their destinations so far. For these traditions to continue, they and the landscapes through which they travel must be protected and cherished. Surely the incredible journeys, that they and other animal travellers make, are some of the most intriguing and awe-inspiring stories in all of nature.

King snakes are constrictors and prey on rodents and reptiles. They even tackle venomous snakes as they have some immunity to their venom. This king snake is polishing off a rattlesnake which nearly equals it in length.

INDEX

Photographic credits

BBC Books would like to thank the following for providing photographs and for permission to reproduce copyright material. While every effort has been made to trace and acknowledge all copyright holders, we would like to apologize should there have been any errors or omissions:

Andrew Anderson 35, 62, 63; Neil Armstrong 86, 95; Jim Borrowman 146-147; Rod Clarke 115, 119, 122-123, 126; Bruce Coleman 19; Louise Dawe-Lane 102; Stephen Dunleavy 90-91, 94, 99, 127; Jeff Foott/NHU 111, 130, 135, 139, 147, 151; John Ford/Ursus Photography 134; Jeff Gee 158, 170-171, 179; Patrice Halley 42, 46, 47, 55, 58, 70-71; Kasuaki Kagii 82; Koji Nakamura 154; NHPA 18, 38, 90, 178, 186; Nature Photographers Ltd 39; Arne C. Nilssen 54; Ben Osborne 6, 150; Oxford Scientific Films 74, 110; Mark Payne-Gill 91, 107; Cherie Pittillo 142, 143; Sinclair Stammers 78; Sinclair Stammers/NHU 79; Matt Thompson 66, 67, 166, 167, 183; Jason Venus 14, 26, 27, 30, 31, 163, 182; Kennan Ward Photography 155.